WITHDRAWN

Jossey–Bass Teacher

Jossey-Bass Teacher provides educators with practical knowledge and tools to create a positive and lifelong impact on student learning. We offer classroom-tested and research-based teaching resources for a variety of grade levels and subject areas. Whether you are an aspiring, new, or veteran teacher, we want to help you make every teaching day your best.

From ready-to-use classroom activities to the latest teaching framework, our value-packed books provide insightful, practical, and comprehensive materials on the topics that matter most to K–12 teachers. We hope to become your trusted source for the best ideas from the most experienced and respected experts in the field.

Hands-On Math Projects with Real-Life Applications

Grades 3–5

Judith A. Muschla and
Gary Robert Muschla

JOSSEY-BASS
A Wiley Imprint
www.josseybass.com

Published by Jossey-Bass
A Wiley Imprint
989 Market Street, San Francisco, CA 94103-1741—www.josseybass.com

Jossey-Bass books and products are available through most bookstores. To contact Jossey-Bass directly call our Customer Care Department within the U.S. at 800-956-7739, outside the U.S. at 317-572-3986, or fax 317-572-4002.

Jossey-Bass also publishes its books in a variety of electronic formats. Some content that appears in print may not be available in electronic books.

ISBN   978-0-4702-6198-9

Printed in the United States of America
FIRST EDITION
PB Printing   10 9 8 7 6 5 4 3 2 1

Contents

Part One: Implementing Math Projects in Your Class

Part Two: The Projects

For Erin

Acknowledgments

We would like to thank our many colleagues for their support, inspiration, and encouragement over the years.

We are grateful to Kate Bradford, our editor at Jossey-Bass, for her support and guidance throughout the entire process of writing this book.

We also thank our daughter, Erin, a math teacher in the Monroe Public School System in New Jersey, for reading through our manuscript, finding our oversights, and offering suggestions.

Our thanks also to Diane Turso for proofreading this book and helping to set it in its final form.

Finally, we thank our students, who have made teaching a rewarding and enjoyable career for us.

About This Book

Competence in mathematics is essential for success in our society. A mere understanding of basic math is no longer enough. Today's students need to be able to think logically; to gather, analyze, and organize data; to make decisions; and to solve complex, multistep problems. They must master high-level critical-thinking skills. Effective math instruction can build the foundation on which such skills can flourish.

To prepare students for the demanding future that awaits them, math teachers must provide a program that shows students how math is used in real life, promotes collaboration, encourages the use of technology, fosters the expression of ideas both orally and in writing, and helps students appreciate that math is not an isolated subject but is connected to other disciplines. The projects presented in this book will help you to achieve these goals.

Math projects offer students many benefits. Perhaps the most important benefit is that when students work on activities based on real-life situations, they see how the math skills they are learning may be applied to the real world. Math projects open the door to bringing other subjects and disciplines into the math class, and students quickly recognize that math is essential to their lives. Math projects also provide students with opportunities to work together cooperatively to solve problems that might be overwhelming for one person to manage. Furthermore, when students collaborate on a project, students of all abilities have the chance to contribute to the solution. Everyone can share in the success.

Hands-On Math Projects with Real-Life Applications, Grades 3–5, consists of two parts. Part One focuses on management and implementation, Part Two contains the math projects. The projects support the Standards and Focal Points of the National Council of Teachers of Mathematics, and they meet the mandates of the No Child Left Behind Act that call for project-based learning, problem-solving strategies in mathematics, and the integration of technology into the classroom.

About the Authors

Judith A. Muschla received her B.A. degree in mathematics from Douglass College at Rutgers University and is certified to teach K–12. She taught math in South River, New Jersey, for more than twenty-five years, at various levels at both South River High School and South River Middle School. In her capacity as a team leader at the middle school, she helped revise the mathematics curriculum to reflect the Standards of the National Council of Teachers of Mathematics, coordinated interdisciplinary units, and conducted math workshops for teachers and parents. She was a recipient of the 1990–1991 Governor's Teacher Recognition Program award in New Jersey, and was named 2002 South River Public School District Teacher of the Year. She has also been a member of the Review Panel for New Jersey's Mathematics Core Curriculum Content Standards.

Gary Robert Muschla received his B.A. and M.A.T. degrees from Trenton State College and taught in Spotswood, New Jersey, for more than twenty-five years. He spent many of those years teaching math at the elementary school level. He has also taught reading and writing and is a successful author. He is a member of the Authors Guild and the National Writers Association. He has written several resources for teachers, among them *Writing Workshop Survival Kit*; *The Writing Teacher's Book of Lists*; *Ready-to-Use Reading Proficiency Lessons and Activities, 10th Grade Level*; *Ready-to-Use Reading Proficiency Lessons and Activities, 8th Grade Level*; *Ready-to-Use Reading Proficiency Lessons and Activities, 4th Grade Level*; *Reading Workshop Survival Kit*; and *English Teacher's Great Books Activities Kit*, all published by Jossey-Bass.

Together, Judith and Gary Muschla have coauthored eight math books published by Jossey-Bass: *The Math Teacher's Problem-a-Day, Grades 4–8*; *Hands-On Math Projects with Real-Life Applications, Grades 6–12*; *The Math Teacher's Book of Lists*; *Math Games: 180 Reproducible Activities to Motivate, Excite, and Challenge Students, Grades 6–12*; *Algebra Teacher's Activities Kit*; *Math Smart! Over 220 Ready-to-Use Activities to Motivate and Challenge Students, Grades 6–12*; *Geometry Teacher's Activities Kit*; and *Math Starters! 5- to 10-Minute Activities to Make Kids Think, Grades 6–12*.

Alignment to the National Council of Teachers of Mathematics Standards and Focal Points

The projects in this book support the Standards and Focal Points of the National Council of Teachers of Mathematics (NCTM), with specific emphasis on the following mathematical processes:

- Problem solving
- Reasoning
- Communication
- Connections
- Representation

An essential part of learning math is problem solving. As students seek the solution to a problem, they must draw on their own knowledge, experience, and skills. They must decide what methods or procedures to use, and they must undertake various actions such as conducting research, analyzing data, organizing information, and drawing conclusions. In their efforts to solve the problem, they reinforce previously learned skills, acquire new skills, and gain greater understanding of mathematics. By presenting students with a variety of practical, engaging problems to solve, you will be supporting the Problem Solving Standard.

As students engage in the math projects contained in this book, they will have the opportunity to make and justify conjectures. By listening to and evaluating the reasoning of their peers, they will hone their own reasoning skills. These and similar actions support the Reasoning Standard.

The projects also support the Communication Standard. Because effective communication depends on clear thought and expression, communication encourages students to think critically, formulate their ideas, and express those ideas with mathematical precision. Communication gives students the opportunity to organize, consolidate, and state their ideas; to consider and evaluate the ideas of others; and to further their understanding of math. An important part of every project in this book is sharing the results of problem solving through formal and informal presentations.

Although students are often taught mathematical skills in isolation or in packets of information, mathematics is a broad, complex subject in which ideas are interconnected and often extend to other disciplines. As students work on projects, they will find relationships between ideas that will broaden their understanding of problems and solutions and help them appreciate how math is interwoven through all parts of the world. Thus, working on math projects supports the Connection Standard.

The projects in this book also support the Representation Standard. Mathematical ideas are represented with notations, symbols, and figures. Typical examples of representations include numbers, expressions, equations, diagrams, charts, tables, and graphs. As students work on projects, they represent mathematical ideas in a variety of ways, which then become the means to explore, model, and develop mathematical concepts. A thorough understanding of mathematical representations will serve students well in their continuing study of math.

Along with supporting the Standards, the projects in this book also adhere to the NCTM Focal Points and Connections to the Focal Points, addressing those areas that are recommended for content emphasis in grades 3–5. The major areas include numbers and operations, algebra, geometry, measurement, and data analysis.

In Table I.1, checkmarks indicate how each project aligns with the NCTM Standards, Focal Points, and Connections to the Focal Points. For some projects, there are no checkmarks for either the Focal Points or their Connections, because the skills in these projects depend on student-selected content.

Table I.1.   Standards Grid

Project Number	Numbers and Operations	Algebra	Geometry	Measurement	Data Analysis	Problem Solving	Reasoning and Proof	Communication	Connections	Representation	Focal Point	Connection to Focal Point
1	√			√		√		√	√	√		√
2			√			√		√	√	√	√	
3	√		√	√	√	√	√	√	√	√	√	
4	√	√				√	√	√	√	√	√	
5	√	√		√	√	√		√	√	√		√
6	√	√		√	√	√		√	√	√	√	
7	√					√		√	√	√	√	
8					√		√	√				
9	√			√	√			√	√	√		√
10	√	√	√	√		√		√	√	√	√	
11					√	√		√	√	√		√
12	√							√	√	√		√
13								√	√	√		
14								√	√			
15								√	√			
16								√				
17								√	√	√		
18						√		√	√	√		
19						√	√	√	√			
20				√		√		√	√	√		

(Continued on next page)

Alignment to the National Council of Teachers of Mathematics Standards

Table I.1. Cont'd

Project Number	Numbers and Operations	Algebra	Geometry	Measurement	Data Analysis	Problem Solving	Reasoning and Proof	Communication	Connections	Representation	Focal Point	Connection to Focal Point
21								√	√	√		
22								√	√	√		
23			√	√		√		√	√	√	√	
24	√		√	√		√	√	√	√	√	√	
25			√	√		√	√			√	√	
26			√	√					√	√	√	
27	√			√	√			√	√	√		√
28	√		√	√		√	√			√	√	
29	√	√				√		√	√	√	√	
30					√	√	√	√	√			
31	√	√			√	√	√	√	√		√	
32			√	√		√	√	√	√			√
33	√	√			√	√	√	√			√	
34	√			√	√	√	√	√	√	√		
35	√							√	√	√		√
36						√	√	√				
37	√					√	√	√				
38								√		√		
39						√	√	√	√	√		
40							√	√		√		

Alignment to the National Council of Teachers of Mathematics Standards

How to Use This Resource

Hands-On Math Projects with Real-Life Applications, Grades 3–5, is divided into two parts. Part One, "Implementing Math Projects in Your Class," contains three chapters devoted to incorporating, managing, and evaluating math projects that will help you use the projects in this book effectively. Chapter One, "An Overview of Using Math Projects," provides specific guidelines for implementing math projects; Chapter Two, "Managing Math Projects," details a variety of classroom management techniques and suggestions; and Chapter Three, "Evaluating Math Projects," offers methods for assessing and grading the work of your students. Each of these chapters includes several lists that summarize information, making it easy for you to find the facts you need. For example, you will find that your role will expand when math projects become a part of your program. Your Role as Teacher and Facilitator, in Chapter One, outlines the many tasks you may assume when your students work on a project.

Each chapter of Part One also includes several reproducibles that can help you establish the classroom routines necessary for the successful implementation of math projects. For example, distributing copies of Chapter Two's Rules for Working in Math Groups, which highlights the behaviors that characterize effective collaboration, will help students to behave appropriately when working together and achieve the goals you set for them.

Part Two contains forty projects divided into six major sections, which is useful for planning interdisciplinary units. The projects provide a broad range of instructional options. Each project stands alone and may be used to introduce, enhance, or conclude a unit or topic. The projects may also be used for enrichment or extra credit. Although many of the projects are designed for students working as partners or in groups, several require students to work individually. Some projects may be completed within two class periods; others may require three or four periods. Several projects may be used as ongoing activities. For example, Project 13, A Class Math Newsletter, in Chapter Six; Project 19, Math Journals, in Chapter Six; or Project 39, Setting up a Math Portfolio, in Chapter Nine may be carried out for a marking period, a semester, or an entire year.

All of the projects follow the same format. First, information for the teacher is presented: background on the topic, goals of the project, the math skills covered, any special materials and equipment that are needed, development, wrap-up, and extensions. This material is followed by a student guide, which offers strategies and suggestions to help students complete the project. Data sheets and worksheets then provide students with additional information or a specialized work space. The student guides, data sheets, and worksheets are numbered according to each project and are reproducible.

We suggest that you use this book as a resource, selecting the projects that will enhance or supplement your curriculum. The forty projects offer a variety of real-life situations that require students to apply specific math skills and that will help them realize the relevance of math in their lives.

We trust that you will find this book to be a valuable resource to your instructional program. Our best wishes to you for a successful and rewarding school year.

Judith and Gary Muschla

Part One

Implementing Math Projects in Your Class

Chapter One

An Overview of Using Math Projects

Computation, problem-solving, and critical-thinking skills are important components of any successful math class. Rather than learning skills in isolation, by working on math projects students study math in context so they can see it applied in real situations. They come to appreciate the importance of math in their lives, and to see the many connections between math and the world.

A successful math project transforms a classroom into a center of learning, collaboration, cooperation, and sharing. The classroom bustles with enthusiasm and activity as students work alone, together, and with the teacher. Along with learning basic math skills, students are encouraged to think logically, analyze data, make decisions, and solve problems that arise from real-life situations, and thus learn and utilize mathematical concepts and skills in meaningful ways.

Your Role as Teacher and Facilitator

To some extent, you must step out of your traditional role when your students work on math projects. In addition to being responsible for introducing concepts, demonstrating skills through example, and grading the work of your students, you will also become a facilitator and promoter. Your goals and methods will broaden. During project work, much of your time will be spent working directly with individuals and groups. As your students work on the projects, you will circulate around the room, offering suggestions, asking questions that lead to insights, and giving encouragement and praise. Sometimes you may simply observe a group's efforts or model appropriate behavior. Occasionally you may need to pull a group back on task. The following list gives some additional components of your new role:

- Organizing and monitoring groups so that your students can work together effectively
- Brainstorming with groups
- Guiding your students in their research efforts
- Offering suggestions to solve problems
- Providing assistance and acting as a resource
- Modeling appropriate behavior and demonstrating skills
- Offering encouragement and applauding efforts
- Explaining that everyone makes mistakes and that mistakes should be viewed as steps to finding solutions
- Helping your students to organize their thoughts as they consider problem-solving strategies
- Showing your students that various strategies may be used to solve the same problem
- Providing time for sharing results

You can incorporate projects into your curriculum in various ways. You can build time for them into your schedule, for example, a period or two each week; or you can reserve time for projects intermittently throughout the year. Some teachers introduce a math project and then give students time to work on it in class over the next few days or after school. Math projects can also be included in an interdisciplinary unit. No matter how you include math projects in your teaching program, however, you should be consistent. Students not only need sufficient time for working on projects, but they also need to know in advance when they will be working on them so they can come to class prepared and ready to work.

Solving Multistep Problems

The problems presented in the math projects contained in this book require skills in computation, analysis, critical thinking, and decision making. Because the types of problems vary, no specific plan for finding solutions applies to all of the problems. You should familiarize your students with various strategies they can use as needed. Explain that strategies are methods or procedures that can be used alone or with other strategies. If a student asks what strategy is best for solving a particular problem, a good answer is, "the one that works best for you." You will likely find that different students will use different strategies to solve the same problem.

Although some of your students may have a knack for problem solving, many will need guidance, and you may wish to distribute copies of the following reproducible: Strategies for Solving Problems. This guide can help students begin their problem-solving efforts and keep them moving forward. There is also much you can do in your regular lessons to help your students acquire sound problem-solving skills. Here's a list of suggestions:

- Assign real-life problems to which your students can relate.
- Present problems that have multiple solutions and that can be solved through several strategies.
- Encourage your students to try various strategies in solving problems.
- Organize your students into cooperative teams.
- Encourage your students to brainstorm for ideas that might lead to solutions.
- Provide problems that have missing information or too much information. Such problems will require students to supply or eliminate data.
- Give problems that connect to other subjects.
- Encourage your students to keep notes on their efforts at solving difficult problems.
- Encourage your students not to give up; persistence is a major factor in successful problem solving.
- Require your students to write explanations of how they solved problems.
- Remind your students always to check answers for logic and accuracy.
- Provide time for discussion and the sharing of solutions.

An essential part of any project is the sharing of solutions and results at the end of an activity. When results are shared, students have the opportunity to hear other viewpoints, to learn about other methods that might have been used to solve problems, and to realize that others may have experienced similar obstacles in solving problems. Not only does sharing help reduce students' feelings that they are the only ones having trouble, it also helps build a sense of class community and fosters an environment that is supportive of problem solving.

Sharing may take many forms. It may be oral, such as a presentation or discussion; written in logs or reports; or illustrated in a drawing, table, or model. Through the various forms of sharing, speaking and writing become essential components of your math class.

Problem solving is hard work, and your students will benefit from your encouragement and advice. Explain that problem-solving skills develop with practice. Just as with anything else—learning to play a musical instrument, excelling at a particular sport, or playing computer games—the more your students work at solving problems, the better they will become. Distribute copies of the reproducible How to Become a Great Problem Solver to highlight some of the characteristics that successful problem solvers share.

Strategies for Solving Problems

There are many ways to solve problems. Following are some strategies.

- Make sure you understand the problem. You may have to read it several times.

- Be sure you understand the question.

- Find the important information in the problems. (Sometimes problems contain facts you do not need.)

- Research and find information.

- Look for patterns, relationships, and connections.

- Use guess and check (also called trial and error).

- Make a table or chart.

- Think logically. Look for connections between ideas and facts.

- Sketch or draw a model to help you "see" the problem better.

- Try to solve a simpler or smaller problem.

- Look at the problem in different ways.

- Estimate. Rounding off numbers can make finding a solution easier. Using whole numbers rather than fractions may help you to see operations more clearly.

- Keep notes as you try to solve the problem. Check your notes to see if you might have missed something.

- Do not give up. Only through hard work can you find answers.

- Double-check your work and make sure your answers make sense.

How to Become a Great Problem Solver

You can become a great problem solver. All it takes is practice. Following are some of the traits of great problem solvers. Try to develop as many of these traits as you can.

Great problem solvers

- Believe they can solve just about any problem.

- Do not give up.

- Try different strategies to solve problems.

- Find important information that helps them solve problems.

- Look at a problem from various viewpoints.

- See patterns, relationships, and connections.

- Are open to new ideas.

- Write notes to keep track of their attempts at solutions.

- Solve problems one step at a time.

- Use their experiences in solving problems.

- Use logic and common sense.

- Double-check their answers.

Developing Math Projects of Your Own

Although this book contains a variety of projects, you, as well as your students, may eventually wish to create projects of your own, designed specifically for the needs of your class. As you develop projects, keep in mind the following points, which will help ensure that students will find the projects stimulating and exciting:

1. Build projects around real-life situations that students will find meaningful.
2. Create projects that capture the interest of your particular students.
3. Be certain that your students possess the mathematical skills necessary to solve any problems in your projects.
4. Develop projects that require analysis, critical thinking, and decision making.
5. Design projects that require students to formulate a plan.

Math projects offer students many benefits. Perhaps the most important benefit is that when students work on problems that are based on real-life situations, they see how the math skills they are learning may be applied to the real world. Math projects open the door to bringing other subjects and disciplines into the math class, and students quickly recognize that math is essential to their lives. Math projects also provide students with the opportunity to work together cooperatively to solve problems that might be overwhelming for one person to manage. Furthermore, when they collaborate on a project, students of all abilities have the chance to contribute to the solution. Everyone can share in the success.

Chapter Two

Managing Math Projects

Successful math projects are the result of effective planning and management. As your students work on projects, they will be engaged in a variety of activities: they will need to gather, analyze, and organize information; confer with each other; examine models; consider different problem-solving strategies; do calculations; and test possible solutions. All of this activity requires a positive classroom environment that fosters inquiry, encourages students to accept responsibility for their learning, and supports both individual and group activities.

Organizing Your Class

There are many ways you can incorporate projects into your class. You may select projects that support a unit you are teaching in math. For example, if your students are studying fractions, Project 24, Picture This (Using Polygons to Model Fractions), can help students see the relationships between fractions as well as sharpen their skills in geometry. Math projects can also enhance programs in other subject areas. If your students are learning about weather in science, Project 5, Weather Observers, can broaden the scope of the topic and give students experience in data analysis.

When you utilize a math project to enhance a unit of instruction, you can build the project into your daily schedule. We suggest you use one class period to explain the overall project, distribute any materials that students might need, organize groups (see the section on organizing math groups provided later in this chapter), and give students twenty minutes or so to plan, brainstorm potential strategies, and get started. Once the project is started, resume your regular math lessons, reserving about twenty minutes at the end of each class for students to continue working on the project. This approach allows you to continue moving forward with the unit. Because not all student groups will finish at the same time, those that finish early may work on extensions of the project, write in math journals, work on challenge or extra-credit activities, or get a head start on homework. When every group is done, schedule a period for sharing results.

Another way to incorporate math projects into your curriculum is to periodically schedule time for them. After you complete a unit, set aside three or four days to work on a project. Some teachers prefer this method because it gives students a break from the routines of the class but does not interfere with the sequence of the general curriculum. Because each of the projects in this book stands alone, each can be used at any time during the year and still provide the benefits of using a variety of skills in meaningful contexts.

Some projects, especially those on which students work individually, may be completed at home. You might give students a choice of these projects as either assignments or bonus activities. Even though in this case the projects are completed on the students' time, you should still provide class time for sharing, because responses to their methods and results from you and their classmates can provide further insight into problem solving.

Building and Maintaining a Positive Classroom Environment

Without question, the environment of a classroom can have either a positive or a negative effect on student attitudes and performance. Enthusiasm thrives in an environment in which people are challenged with interesting problems, are not afraid to risk making mistakes, and are encouraged to share their ideas. The tone you set in your classroom, your expectations, and the procedures you maintain are the foundations for such an environment. Although there is much you can do to promote the success of the students in your class, your students must also be willing to make the class a success. This is particularly true during group activities, when your students must accept more responsibility than what is normally expected of them in the traditional class. As they work on math projects, they must remain focused. This is not a time to talk about who might be named lead in the class play or about what the students will do after school. Talk to them about your expectations concerning their participation in the project when you first explain the project's goals.

The best classes are founded on a spirit of cooperation and energetic intellectual pursuit and on the belief that math can be learned by all. Math classes that have a positive learning environment share many of the following characteristics:

- The goals of the teacher for the class are realistic. They are high enough so that students must work hard, but they are not so high that students feel frustrated.
- The atmosphere of the classroom is one of openness, fresh ideas, and sharing.
- A major tenet of the class is that everyone can learn math.
- The classroom is bright and cheerful.
- The classroom routines foster inquiry and problem solving.
- The classroom has clear, orderly procedures. Students behave appropriately and follow the classroom rules.
- The rules of the classroom are fair and consistent.
- Students are aware of the goals and objectives of the class.

- Evaluation is reasonable and fair.
- Along with providing instruction in math, the teacher guides and encourages students.
- The teacher models problem solving and supports students in finding solutions.
- Math is connected to real-life problems and situations.
- Cooperation in learning is encouraged.
- Sufficient time is provided for problem solving.
- Students use various strategies to solve problems.
- Students explain their reasoning during problem solving.
- Manipulatives are used whenever possible to show students relationships between mathematical concepts.
- Sharing of results is encouraged.
- Calculators and computers are used in problem solving.
- The work of students is prominently displayed.
- Math is related to other subjects as much as possible.
- Students appreciate the importance of mathematics in their lives.

If your students are to work efficiently on math projects, they will need the classroom's physical arrangement to support problem solving. Tables are desirable, but if you do not have tables, you can push desks together. Provide enough room between groups so that each group can work without distracting the other groups. There should also be enough work area for students to gather to discuss possible strategies, analyze data, examine models, and work on calculations.

Support problem solving in whatever ways you can. Always look for ways to highlight problem-solving strategies, interesting facts and articles about math that focus on problem solving, and the work of your students that illustrates problem solving. Use bulletin boards, corridor display cases, and media center exhibits to draw attention to your program and the accomplishments of your students.

Suggestions for Presenting and Implementing Projects

Although every teacher has his or her own teaching style, techniques, and methods, we have found that the following plan offers a helpful structure for presenting and implementing math projects. The plan can be divided into three parts: *introduction, work time,* and *wrapping up.*

Introduction

Start a math project by explaining the situation and any problems that are to be solved. Give your students examples, review any concepts or skills they will need to solve the problems, and relate the project to real-life scenarios as much as possible. Encourage your students to ask any questions they might have. Having a student paraphrase the project and what needs to be solved can clarify what everyone is to do.

When you feel sure that the students understand the basic project, distribute copies of the student guide and discuss the information presented there. Any data sheets, worksheets, and additional materials should also be distributed at this time. Having everything they need before they begin helps students to see the full scope of the project.

Work Time

As your students work in their groups, circulate around the room offering advice and encouragement. This is also a time to monitor and model student behavior.

Provide guidance as necessary to keep students from wandering off the topic. If you see this happening, point out where the students are getting off track, or suggest that they move in another direction. However, do not give answers to any problems. If your students feel that you will provide answers, they will be less inclined to do the hard work and thinking that will result in finding the answers themselves. To encourage students to find their own answers, some teachers prefer to be asked a question only after the question has been presented to the other members of the group or to a partner and no one else has been able to answer it.

As you observe your students, you may find that a group is having trouble moving forward. In such cases, have the students restate the point of the project and break it down into parts to isolate the most important facts. Other groups may understand the project but have trouble finding effective strategies that will lead to solutions. Suggest that the students in these groups brainstorm various strategies and examine each one to see if it leads to a possible solution.

As you move around the room, note the interactions of the members of each group. No matter how carefully you structure the groups, in just about every class and during any given project some groups will work well together, others will be dominated by one or two members, and some will just be unmotivated. When a group is working well, it is best to leave it alone. Working on a math project is a time for students to discover their own solutions. If, however, a group is not working well, you should sit in on it and model appropriate behavior. Make sure that everyone participates, and encourage the group's members to help one another. If necessary, assume the role of group leader to get things going, then gradually fade into the background as the students begin to assume ownership of the project. You may find that you must often remind some students of the proper procedures and behavior, especially during the first few weeks of class.

Wrapping Up

Sharing is vital to the successful culmination of a math project. Discussing methods and results helps students to realize that some problems have multiple solutions that may be discovered through various strategies. This is an important lesson for students. In the real world, many problems have several solutions and can be solved in many ways. For more information on sharing, see the section on sharing results presented later in this chapter.

Conferences with Individuals and Groups

In most cases, conferences with students are integrated into a project and conducted during the students' work time. Conferences may focus on progress, procedures, or specific questions and may last only a minute or two. The purpose of any conference is to help students better understand the project on which they are working, as well as to help them improve their understanding of mathematics. Often students may need only an answer to a simple question. In such instances, provide the necessary guidance and let them get back to work. However, if an individual or group has encountered an obstacle, use it as your starting point for the conference.

Direct each conference to solving a particular problem or using a specific skill. Attempting to do too much at once may confuse students. During the conference keep your tone positive, encourage student participation, and offer specific suggestions. You may need to point a group in the right direction, toward finding more information; offer encouragement to a group that is about to give up; or assure a group that their efforts are worthwhile.

Any praise you give to students should be genuine, because they can always tell when it is not. Be careful not to make any negative or sarcastic remarks. The conference should be a time of support and should help students complete the project correctly.

The Importance of Cooperation

In many occupations, people work in teams and groups, and the experience your students gain now working together on math projects will serve them not only in your class but in the future as well. Cooperation fosters inquiry and discussion, and students often learn more when working together than when trying to solve a complicated problem alone. Cooperative learning also provides students with the opportunity to acquire valuable social skills.

Students working in groups are more likely than students working alone to take active roles in class activities. Because the group can provide support, it is easier to get involved. When students see other group members struggling with the same problems, they often feel less intimidated about offering their thoughts, and many students who are hesitant to share ideas with the whole class will share them with their group. Moreover, when students offer suggestions toward the solution of a problem, they receive immediate feedback from the other group members. Such sharing frequently results in a discussion of math that is both stimulating and useful.

Groups working on math projects become involved in a variety of activities. Group members need to discuss and assign tasks, consider how to solve problems, try different strategies, collect and analyze data, reach solutions, and decide how to justify and share results. Working together in a group helps build student confidence, promotes critical thinking, and results in a sense of ownership of the project.

Organizing Math Groups

Although the ideal math group is composed of random students, you should always be mindful of achieving balance and cooperation when forming groups. Groups of three to five generally work well for many projects. Larger groups may become somewhat unwieldy, especially if one or two of the students are overly energetic. If a group is too small for a complex project, it is sometimes hard for students to generate enough ideas.

An easy way to make random groups is simply to count down your roster in sets of three, four, or five and assign the numbers to students. Before announcing the groups to the students, however, review the list of members and make sure you have a mix of abilities as well as of gender and ethnicity. You might also consider factors such as readiness, learning style, and interest levels. It is a good idea to avoid having best friends or students who do not get along in the same group. Make any final changes before informing the students about the groups.

You should also change the membership in your groups periodically. Rearranging groups allows students to interact with different personalities and to be exposed to different viewpoints. In the real world, people are often required to work with others whose outlooks and abilities are quite different from their own. When making new groups, you can just switch some members from each of the existing groups into other groups (note that switching only one member keeps too much of the original group together), or you might prefer to create entirely new groups for every project.

Once you have arranged your groups, explain to your students the need for working together. Suggest that a group might work most efficiently when tasks are divided. You may also suggest that students assume various roles that will help define responsibilities. For example, one student might serve as group leader, whose purpose is to keep the group on task and guide it toward the solution of the problem. Another student might be the recorder, whose responsibility includes writing down the group's ideas, strategies, and conclusions.

Unless your students have worked in groups before, they will probably need training in the procedures of effective group work. Distributing copies of the list of Rules for Working in Math Groups, provided later in this section, can be helpful in discussing expected behavior. During the first project, focus much of your attention on group interaction. You will likely need to model behavior and remind your students of procedures often, especially in the beginning of the year. Monitor the groups and show them how to act and behave. Acquiring the skills necessary for effective group work may take them a few weeks.

Working cooperatively in groups offers students an excellent way to learn math. The following summary of the key points discussed in this section can help you to organize your math groups:

- Groups should consist of from three to five students.
- Organize your groups randomly, but realize that you may need to adjust group membership to ensure that students work well together.

- Change your group membership periodically. This gives students the chance to interact with others and to experience new work relationships.
- Always explain the purpose of group work and the expected behaviors. Some students may have little experience working in groups, particularly on math projects.
- Because groups often benefit from a division of labor, consider having students assume specific roles, including the following:
  - Leader: guides the group toward its goal and makes sure everyone stays on task
  - Recorder: keeps notes of the group's ideas, strategies, and solutions
  - Checker: reviews the work of the group
  - Materials monitor: assumes responsibility for any materials the group uses
  - Presenter: shares the group's findings with other members of the class

Note: Students may assume more than one role.

Rules for Working in Math Groups

The following rules can help your group work together. Each member of the group should

- Behave properly.

- Work with other group members.

- Help others.

- Share his or her ideas.

- Give others a chance to speak.

- Listen carefully and politely when others are speaking.

- Ask questions when he or she does not understand something.

- Keep the discussion on the math project.

- Discuss ideas calmly.

- Do the best that he or she can.

Sharing Results

Sharing results is crucial to doing the projects. When students become aware of other strategies, solutions, and approaches, their understanding of math broadens. Sharing may take the form of an oral report; a presentation incorporating charts, tables, or models; or a written log or summary.

At the culmination of each project, provide time for each group to share its methods and findings with the rest of the class. Each group can either designate one presenter or have different students present different parts of the project. While one group is presenting, the rest of the class should pay attention and think about any questions they may have, but explain that they should hold their questions until the presentation is done. Encourage students to discuss successful strategies as well as strategies that did not work. It is possible that other groups tried the same strategies but got different results or experienced different problems. The more math is discussed, the more opportunities students will have to gain new insights and understand concepts.

After the students in each group have completed their presentation, encourage questions from the class. All of the members of the group may help to answer the questions, but only one student should speak at a time. This is also the time for members of other groups to offer comments or observations. Emphasize that any discussion should be positive.

If the members of a group need help presenting their results, guide the students in reporting the strategies they used—their methods, procedures, and solutions. Consider asking such questions as the following:

- How did your group divide tasks?
- What strategies did you discuss?
- What strategies did you try?
- What kinds of data did you need to gather?
- What sources did you use for finding information?
- What problems, or obstacles, did you run into?
- How do you know your findings are correct?
- Are there other possible solutions? If yes, what are they? Which one is most valid?

Always provide enough time for all groups to share their results. After sharing is finished, summarize the project and the results obtained by the various groups. Highlight any unusual strategies or problems encountered, and be sure to discuss how the mathematics used applies to life.

The Importance of Writing in Math Class

The value of writing in math classes is well documented. Writing offers students opportunities for examining and sharing their thoughts about mathematics in a formalized manner. Through writing, students can connect new ideas with concepts they have already learned, summarize their understanding of math, and communicate their thoughts to others. Only when we truly understand something can we explain it and put it clearly into words.

Many types of writing can be done during math class. In addition to writing reports and about how to solve specific problems, students can also write entries in math journals. Chapter Six includes several projects that focus on integrating math and language arts.

Encourage students to share their thoughts about math concepts, methods, and applications through writing. Guide them in their writing efforts to choose meaningful topics and think carefully about what they are writing.

Perhaps your students have already learned about a method of writing called the writing process. There are various stages to this process, from the formulation of ideas through writing, rewriting, editing, and publishing (or sharing). Making students aware of the ways in which writers actually work can support them in their own writing. To help your students understand the writing process, distribute copies of the following reproducible: Math and the Writing Process, and discuss with them the stages of the process.

Hands-On Math Projects

Math and the Writing Process

Writing can be broken down into various stages or steps called the writing process. Authors go through these stages when they write. Understanding this process can help you with your own writing.

Stage 1: Prewriting
- Thinking of a purpose
- Thinking of ideas
- Brainstorming
- Researching and gathering facts
- Analyzing ideas
- Organizing ideas
- Focusing ideas

Stage 2: Drafting
- Writing
- Changing ideas
- Expanding ideas

Stage 3: Revising
- Rewriting
- Rethinking, changing, deleting, or adding information
- Clarifying ideas
- Checking ideas and math facts
- Doing more research

Stage 4: Editing
- Making any final corrections, including those relating to math
- Proofreading

Stage 5: Publishing or Sharing
- Sharing your written work with others
- Making copies of your work
- Displaying your work

Using Technology in Math Projects

Technology is essential for teaching, learning, and doing math. Devices such as calculators and computers are especially helpful for working on math projects because they enable students to collect, analyze, and organize data; view dynamic images of math models; and perform computations with accuracy and efficiency. The skills for working with technology that your students learn in school will serve them throughout their lives.

Calculators

Calculators are an important part of any math class. By freeing students from the slow work of manual computation, they allow more time for investigation, reasoning, decision making, and problem solving. Calculators can be particularly helpful to students who have trouble with computation. These students often become so worried about the basic operations that they are unable to share fully in many of the other aspects of project work, such as collaboration, gathering and analyzing data, and making decisions. Because calculators enable students to focus on problem solving rather than on computation, they can help your students attend to the math projects themselves rather than just to the calculations. If calculators are a part of your program, make certain that students know how to use them correctly.

Computers

Computers also can assume a major role in project work. They can be used for research, to provide visual images of mathematical concepts and ideas, and to link students to math Web sites throughout the world. They can also help with data collection and analysis. Moreover, they can be used to write reports and to print results.

Although many of your students will likely possess general computer skills, you should assume that most of them will not have had much experience using technology to solve multistep problems. Incorporating computers into your program will offer significant benefits. Not only will your students learn the skills necessary to utilize the equipment, but they will also be able to use computers to support their efforts in problem solving.

If your school employs a computer specialist who works with students, meet with her and discuss the needs of your students. Perhaps she can include the utilization of computers for math projects and problem solving into her instructional program. If your school does not have a technology or computer specialist who works with students, you will have to provide your students with the training they need yourself.

Although you do not have to be a computer expert, you should be familiar enough with the hardware and software so you can demonstrate their basic use to your students. If necessary, ask your school's technology specialist to show you how to use computers and their software to support math projects. Also, most technology comes with tutorials that can show you the basics.

Many students today use computers at home and are able to learn to operate new applications quite readily. (Some may even have more computer skills than you.) Consider organizing your students into groups by placing one or two students who possess strong computer skills with those whose technical skills may be weak. The students with technical skills will take the lead with the technology, thus reducing any anxiety that other members of the group might have about working with the equipment. Monitor the groups closely, however, to ensure that the less technically minded do in fact gain experience working with the equipment and applications.

The Internet

The Internet is a vast medium of information and can be a valuable research asset as your students work on math projects. In addition, countless interactive Web sites devoted to math offer tests, quizzes, and problem-solving activities. Incorporating the use of the Internet into your math program can greatly expand the scope of student learning.

Being able to search the Internet for information is an essential skill that will be useful to students far beyond math class. Unless they know the Web address of a particular site that is likely to provide the information they are seeking, they will have to conduct a search using a search engine such as Google or Ask.

Your school district may have specific guidelines regarding what search engines to use, but if it does not, http://kids.yahoo.com, a part of Yahoo!, contains an excellent search engine for young students. In addition, the site has a section called Studyzone. If you click on math in this section, you will get a list of some of the best math sites for students (as determined by Yahoo!'s editors).

Internet search engines can help you find information on just about anything. The key to finding the information you need is to use search engines effectively. Using precise search terms yields precise results, and using general terms yields general results. For example, searching on *square* will provide more accurate results than searching on *figure*.

On the surface, a math class in which students are engaged in math projects appears to be quite different from a traditional math class. However, these seemingly different models have much in common. In both models, students learn math, procedures must be followed, and motivation is crucial; but a class working on math projects greatly exceeds in activities and learning what is common to the traditional class. Math projects demonstrate to students the connections between math and other subjects, and they offer students the chance to incorporate various skills, strategies, and methods into finding solutions to meaningful problems. Most significant is that math projects help show students the broad scope of mathematics and its far-reaching importance in their lives.

Chapter Three

Evaluating Math Projects

Evaluation is an essential part of the learning process. Through evaluation, teachers can determine the effectiveness of their instruction and assess their students' understanding of mathematics.

When evaluating your students' work on math projects, you may utilize a variety of tools, some of the most useful being observation logs, checklists, and point systems. Because these evaluative methods are flexible, you can use the ones that best satisfy your needs. Combining the evaluation of math projects with the tests, quizzes, classwork, and homework of the general curriculum can give you a detailed profile of your students' overall achievement in math.

Observation Logs

As you circulate around the classroom while your students work on math projects, you can observe them working individually or in groups. Writing down your observations will provide you with a permanent record of their progress. A practical way to do this is to use either the Individual Observation Log or the Group Observation Log, both of which are provided here.

INDIVIDUAL OBSERVATION LOG

Name _____

Project _____

Date	Comments

GROUP OBSERVATION LOG

Names _____

Project _____

Date	Comments

It is unrealistic to try to write a detailed account of every student every day. Limiting your observations to five to ten students per day can reduce your workload to a manageable level. Attach individual log sheets to a clipboard that you can carry around the room, and focus your attention on the students you wish to observe. You may later transfer your observations to your grade book or to a grading program on your computer.

When entering information onto the logs, record indicators of your students' mathematical thinking, understanding of concepts, or insights. You might also note behavior. Concentrating on two or three skills or behaviors reduces the chance that you will feel overwhelmed with things to look for. It is helpful to develop your own system of shorthand using abbreviations, codes, and phrases for recording observations. For example:

- Identify names with initials, for example, James becomes *J*.
- Abbreviate words used frequently, such as:

excellent	ex
good	g
fair	f
well	w
strategy	strat
work	wk
process	proc
question	quest
group	gp
illustrate	il
problem	prob
needs improvement	ni

- Use phrases whenever possible.

Here is a sample entry on an individual log: "Wked w with gp. Offered strat to solve prob."

Individual and group conferences provide opportunities to gain understanding of your students' growth in mathematics. Simply speaking with students about the project on which they are working can give you insight into their thoughts, feelings, and understanding of math.

Although you can learn much about your students when they ask you questions, you can also ask them specific questions that will help show their understanding of math. Such questions may focus on comprehension of problems, formulation of strategies, procedures, calculations, justification of solutions, relationships between ideas, or group cooperation. Preparing a list of questions ahead of time can help you concentrate on the points you wish to address. Because frequently many of the students in a class have the same problems and concerns, asking a few students the same questions will often provide information about the thinking of the class in general. Following is a list of questions you can ask during observations and conferences.

Questions for Observations

Asking students questions about their work can provide you with insight about their progress. Following are just some of the questions you might decide to ask:

- What is the question in this problem? How would you explain this problem and its question to a friend?

- What information must you have before you can find a solution?

- Does this problem have any information you do not need? What is it and why is it not needed?

- How are the facts of this problem connected? How does one fact relate to another? Do the facts form a pattern?

- What strategies might you try to solve this problem? Which strategy do you think is the best? Why?

- Might a sketch or drawing help you solve the problem? If yes, how?

- How might your group divide tasks in solving this problem?

- What is the best solution to the problem?

- How can you justify your solution?

Checklists

Checklists are another useful tool for observation. Unlike an observation log, on which you write notes regarding the progress of the student, a checklist contains predetermined skills and behaviors. As you observe one of the skills or behaviors on your list in a particular student, you simply check it off. As with the observation log, it is most practical to select five to ten students per day on whom to focus your attention. Although a checklist may include numerous skills, it may be best to concentrate on only a few, selecting those that apply to particular projects.

A sample Skills Checklist is included here. You may use it in its current form or as a reference for designing your own. It is set up for five days. It also provides space for comments should you wish to record an observation in more detail.

SKILLS CHECKLIST

Name _____

Project _____

| E = exceptional | S = satisfactory | N = needs improvement |

Skill	Date				
Understands problem					
Finds useful strategies					
Implements strategies					
Collects needed data					
Eliminates unnecessary data					
Organizes data					
Analyzes data					
Finds relationships					
Uses models					
Tests strategies					
Explains results orally					
Explains results in writing					
Justifies solutions					
Uses logic in arguments					
Makes estimates					
Makes accurate calculations					
Uses technology					
Works cooperatively					
Supports group members					
Shares ideas with others					
Listens to others' ideas					
Remains on task					
Is persistent					
Demonstrates creativity					
Shows enthusiasm					
Tries new ideas					
Takes risks					
Is confident					
Comments:					

Many teachers are required to maintain numerical scores or grades for their students' work. Because most math projects are complex activities, it is usually not fair to base students' grades simply on completion. A system in which points are assigned to specific parts of the project is an alternative.

Although you can break down point totals to fit your personal grading criteria, the following point system works well for most projects. It is based on a total of 100 points, which can be easily translated into percentages.

Grading Projects on a Point System

Following is an example of how the parts of a math project can be broken down and quantified. The total number of points is 100. You may use this system as it is presented or as a reference for designing your own system. The system may be applied to the group as a whole—when all members of the group earn the same grade—or it may be modified to determine individual grades. To assess individuals, the last two criteria—*persistence* and *cooperation*—can be evaluated on the basis of your observation of individual students.

- *Solution/results:* 25 points

  The solution is valid and practical.

- *Justification of results:* 15 points

  The students backed up their results with reasonable arguments.

- *Methods:* 15 points

  The students considered various strategies. They eliminated unnecessary facts and found the necessary information. They analyzed and organized their information. They used technology where applicable.

- *Accuracy:* 15 points

  Reasoning was logical and clear. Computation was accurate.

- *Creativity:* 10 points

  The students showed insightful thinking.

- *Persistence:* 10 points

  The students did not give up.

- *Cooperation:* 10 points

  The students worked well together, shared ideas, and listened to one another's ideas.

Evaluating Writing

Because the standards of the National Council of Teachers of Mathematics emphasize the importance of communication, writing should be an integral part of any math curriculum. When your students write about math, they share with you much of their understanding of and attitudes toward math.

Writing is a significant part of many math projects. Over the course of a school year you may evaluate various types of student writing, including articles, essays, reports, explanations of solved problems, biographies of mathematicians, written logs of problem solving, and simple ponderings over those "tough" problems. The exception here is math journals; we recommend that you do not grade journals. They are storehouses of a student's thoughts, reflections, and impressions about math (see Project 19). Once you start grading journals, many students will write what they think you want to see in hopes of achieving a higher grade. When that happens, you will no longer find the honesty that can be so valuable and refreshing in journals.

When you grade your students' writing, select a few criteria on which to focus. This approach will make it easier to keep your objectivity. Discuss these criteria with your students before they start writing. Also, rather than taking home a pile of papers to read each night, take only a workable number. If you try to do too much, you will become frustrated and probably lose perspective. Write comments to your students on their writing, particularly on how they address math ideas and issues. Keep your comments upbeat and positive. When criticism is necessary, be sure it contains suggestions for improvement. The following list provides additional suggestions for grading writing.

Grading Writing in Math Class

Grading students' math writing can be new territory for many teachers. The following ideas can help:

- Before the assignment, discuss with your students what you will be looking for when you evaluate their writing.

- Encourage your students to edit one another's writing and to revise their work before handing it in.

- Concentrate your evaluation on the overall paper, but comment on only one or two points. Mentioning more may only confuse or discourage students.

- Write your comments and responses directly on the students' papers whenever possible.

- Keep your comments positive, and offer specific suggestions for improvement.

Following is a model for scoring student writing, based on percentages:

Focus	All ideas in the writing support the topic.	20%
Content	The student uses fresh, insightful, or original ideas. The topic is developed and supported with details. The math is correct, and shows an understanding of concepts.	25%
Organization	The writing is developed logically from beginning to end. An introduction, body, and conclusion can be identified.	25%
Style	The writing flows and ideas are communicated effectively.	15%
Mechanics	The writer uses correct punctuation, grammar, and spelling.	15%

Student Self-Evaluation

Honest self-evaluation is perhaps the most valuable form of evaluation. Although virtually all students expect their learning to be evaluated by their teachers, few have ever been asked to evaluate themselves.

Encourage your students to evaluate their own progress. A good place to record thoughts about personal growth in math is in math journals (see Project 19). At the end of a project, ask your students to write a journal entry about the project. Suggest that they include the strategies they used, the problems they encountered, and what they learned from the project.

If you prefer, you may distribute copies of the following Student Self-Evaluation. Having students answer these questions will help them to evaluate their own work and learning.

Student Self-Evaluation

Project Title: _____

Answer the following questions about this project:

1. What did I like about this project? _____

_____

_____

2. What did I not like about this project? _____

_____

_____

3. What strategies did I use to complete the project? _____

_____

_____

4. Could I have used other strategies? If yes, which ones? _____

_____

_____

5. What problems did I have in finding a solution? _____

_____

_____

_____

6. What did I learn during this project? _____

_____

_____

As teachers, we continuously evaluate the achievement of our students, yet it is equally important for us to step back occasionally and evaluate our own achievement. This is particularly true for teachers who are implementing projects for the first time. At the very least, you should evaluate yourself by considering what went well and what you would do differently next time. Asking yourself the questions contained in the following Teacher Self-Evaluation can be helpful.

Evaluation is clearly an essential part of the program of any classroom. To be effective, it should be continuous and fair, because its overall purpose is to foster and assist learning.

Teacher Self-Evaluation

Answering the following questions can help ensure that your next project will be even more successful.

- Did I present the project effectively? Were my directions and explanations clear? If not, how might I make them clearer next time?

- Did the students understand what they were supposed to do? How might I help them understand better?

- Did I set up the classroom appropriately? What could I change to make the classroom more suitable for working on math projects?

- Were the students organized into effective groups? How might I have re-arranged the groups to make them more effective?

- Did the students work efficiently? Was their behavior appropriate? How might I help them to improve their behavior?

- Did I monitor learning effectively? Do I know what each student learned?

- Did I ask good questions that provided guidance without giving away answers? What was my best question? What was my least effective question?

- Did I provide enough time for sharing and discussion upon conclusion of the project? If not, how might I provide more time in the schedule next time?

- What might I do to improve this project?

Part Two

The Projects

Chapter Four

Math and Science

Earth by the Numbers

WHEN STUDENTS THINK OF MATH, they usually think of the basic operations and computation. They do not think about the many ways we use math to describe our world. This project helps students relate math to the way we look at the Earth.

Goal

Working in groups of three or four, students will describe features of the Earth using numbers. They will select some aspect of their findings and display their data in the form of a chart, table, graph, or drawing. *Suggested time:* two to three class periods.

Skills Covered

1. Using measurements
2. Using the concepts of *circumference, diameter, square miles,* and *miles per hour*
3. Researching facts about the Earth from a mathematical perspective
4. Expressing mathematical information in the form of a chart, table, graph, or drawing
5. Communicating mathematical findings
6. Using technology (if computers are used)

Special Materials and Equipment

Reference books, such as atlases, earth science books, and geography books; poster paper; rulers; markers and crayons. Optional: computers with Internet access and printers.

Development

- Ask your students what they think of when you say *math* or *mathematics*. Most will probably say they think of addition, subtraction, multiplication, and division. Some may think of word problems or problem solving. It is unlikely that many will think of using math to describe the world.
- Start this project by explaining to your students that they will work in groups and that they will describe various details of the Earth with numbers. For example, without numbers we could not compare the heights of mountains or the lengths of rivers, or measure the distance from one place to another.
- Distribute copies of Student Guide 1.1 and review the information on it with your students. Emphasize that they are to represent their findings with a table, chart, graph, or drawing.
- Hand out copies of Worksheet 1.2: Earth Extremes. Go over the information with your students. Note that the worksheet contains various details about the Earth. The students are to research these details and describe them with numbers.
- Encourage your students to use a variety of reference books. If possible, reserve time in the school's library for your students to conduct research. Consult with the librarian in advance so she can set aside the reference materials your students will need. If your students have online access, suggest that they search for information on the Internet. They should use such search terms as *longest river, highest mountain,* and *fastest sea animal.*
- Emphasize that after your students have completed the given items on Worksheet 1.2, they are to identify between five and ten other details of the Earth and describe these items with numbers. This part of the project is wide open. You might suggest that students find extremes for plants—for example, the tallest tree in the world—extremes of weather, or extremes for a specific continent.
- Explain to your students that once they have completed Worksheet 1.2 and obtained their additional details, they are to choose some of the data they found and illustrate it with a chart, table, graph, or drawing. Note that they have much latitude in deciding what data they will highlight and how they will illustrate it. For example, they might create a graph showing the elevations of the five highest mountains of the world. The data they choose to represent should be related in some way and should be accurate.
- Remind your students that they are to present their findings to the class, so they should appoint a spokesperson. The presentation should focus on the representation of their data and on the extremes they have selected.

Answer Key for Worksheet 1.2

Some of the following answers are approximations, and some answers may vary according to source. For example, students may find sources that identify killer whales as the fastest sea mammal, able to attain speeds of nearly thirty-five miles per hour, while other sources claim that the blue whale is the fastest, able to reach speeds of thirty miles per hour. If your students find different answers for some items, discuss why this might be and how they can solve the apparent confusion by checking additional sources.

Planetary facts: (1) 7,926 miles; (2) 25,000 miles; (3) 93 million miles; (4) $365\frac{1}{4}$, 1 year; (5) 24 hours, 1 day

Some geographical extremes of the Earth: (1) Mt. Everest (Asia), 29,035 feet; (2) Pacific Ocean, 64 million square miles; (3) Nile River (Africa), 4,145 miles; (4) Roe River, Montana, USA, 201 feet; (5) Sahara Desert, Africa, 3.5 million square miles

Some animal extremes of the Earth: (1) blue whale, 110 feet, 210 tons; (2) African elephant, 13 feet high, 8 tons; (3) giraffe, 19 feet; (4) ostrich, 9 feet, 345 pounds; (5) bee hummingbird, 2 inches, 0.5 ounce; (6) koala, 22 hours a day; (7) box turtle, 100 years; (8) cheetah, 70 miles per hour; (9) sailfish, 68 miles per hour; (10) dragonfly, 36 miles per hour

Wrap Up

Have your students share their results with the class. Discuss the strategies they used for finding information, and why they illustrated their data in the manner in which they did. Display their work.

Extension

Suggest that your students research and describe various details of your state or region of the country using numbers.

Copyright © 2009 by Judith A. and Gary Robert Muschla

STUDENT GUIDE 1.1

Earth by the Numbers

Project

Your group is to describe details of the Earth using numbers. You will create a table, chart, graph, or drawing to highlight some of your results.

Key Steps

1. Complete Worksheet 1.2 first. Use reference books for research; almanacs, atlases, science books, and geography books will be helpful. If possible, search the Internet for information.

2. Divide your research efforts among the group. Different members of the group should find information about different topics.

3. Brainstorm with your group to identify other details of the Earth you will describe with numbers. Choose some of your findings and illustrate them with a chart, table, graph, or drawing. Be sure to include the math facts.

4. Choose a spokesperson to share your findings with the class. Be ready to explain why you illustrated your findings the way you did. For example, why did you create a chart instead of a graph?

Special Tips

- Keep accurate notes on where you found your information. This will make it easy to recheck information if you have to.

- Some examples of other details of the Earth to describe with numbers include the following:

  - The hottest and coldest places
  - The highest and lowest temperatures recorded
  - The tallest or biggest plants
  - The biggest snake or smallest frog
  - The fastest sea mammal

To Be Submitted

Your completed worksheet

Your chart, table, graph, or drawing

Name _____   Date _____

Earth Extremes

We use numbers to describe the Earth. In fact, it would be hard to describe our planet without numbers. Find the following number facts about the world. Then find five to ten other facts that you can describe with numbers.

Some Planetary Facts

1. Diameter of the Earth: _____

2. Circumference of the Earth: _____

3. The Earth's average distance from the sun: _____

4. Number of days it takes the Earth to revolve around the sun:

   _____ = 1 _____

5. Time it takes the Earth to spin once on its axis:

   _____ = 1 _____

Some Geographical Extremes of the Earth

1. Highest mountain and its elevation: _____

2. Biggest ocean and its size (in square miles): _____

3. Longest river and its length: _____

4. Shortest river and its length: _____

5. Biggest desert and its size (in square miles): _____

Earth Extremes *(Cont'd.)*

Some Animal Extremes of the Earth

1. Biggest animal, its length and weight: _____

2. Biggest land animal, its height and weight: _____

3. Tallest animal and its height: _____

4. Biggest bird and its size: _____

5. Smallest bird and its size: _____

6. Animal that sleeps the most and amount of sleep: _____

7. Animal that lives longest and number of years: _____

8. Fastest land animal and its speed: _____

9. Fastest ocean fish and its speed: _____

10. Fastest insect and its speed: _____

Other Examples of Extremes (5 to 10):

_____

_____

_____

_____

_____

_____

_____

_____

_____

Geometry All Around Us

FOR MOST STUDENTS, geometry occurs only in math class. It is limited to classwork and homework, with an occasional special activity. Most of them do not see the relevance of geometry in their daily lives. This project can help your students gain a glimpse of how geometry relates to the natural as well as to the man-made world.

Goal

Working in groups of three or four, students will create a collage showing examples of geometry in the world. They will also write a brief description of their collages, highlighting examples of geometric shapes and principles. *Suggested time:* two to three class periods.

Skills Covered

1. Identifying examples of polygons and other geometric shapes in the natural and man-made world
2. Classifying line segments as parallel or perpendicular
3. Classifying two-dimensional shapes by their sides and angles
4. Communicating math ideas
5. Using technology (if computers are used)
6. Identifying line and rotational symmetry (optional)

Special Materials and Equipment

Old magazines and newspapers; reference books, such as almanacs and atlases; scissors; poster paper; glue and transparent tape; rulers; pencils, markers, crayons, and colored pencils. Optional: computers with Internet access and printers.

Development

- This project is an excellent supplement to a unit on geometry because it focuses on lines, angles, polygons, circles, and three-dimensional figures. A few weeks before beginning the project, start collecting old magazines and newspapers that students can use in making their collages. You might ask students and colleagues to bring some in. (To protect privacy, be sure to remove any address labels before distributing the materials.) Perhaps your school's media specialist or librarian has old magazines he or she can give you. Keep a cardboard box or milk crate in class for storing the materials until they are needed.

- Present this project according to the abilities of your students. Focus the attention of younger students on basic figures such as lines, angles, squares, rectangles, triangles, and circles. If your students are older and have a strong background in geometry, include polygons, such as pentagons and hexagons; parallel and perpendicular lines; spirals; arcs; and symmetry.

- Begin this project by explaining to your students that they will work in groups to create a collage that shows examples of geometry in the world. (If necessary, explain that a collage is an arrangement of pictures on a specific theme.) If you have an example of a collage, show it to your students so they can see what they are to make.

- Hand out copies of Student Guide 2.1 and go over the information it provides with your students. Explain that they are to find or draw pictures for their collages.

- Distribute copies of Data Sheet 2.2: Geometry Everywhere. Discuss the examples given on the sheet. (If your students are unfamiliar with many of the terms on this sheet, you may prefer to generate a different list of examples with the class.) Direct the attention of your students to a corner of the classroom. Point out the parallel and perpendicular lines of the walls and ceiling as well as the right angles formed at the corners. Note any other examples of geometry around the classroom, for example, a circular clock, square tiles, and rectangular doors and windows. Also be sure to mention examples of geometry in the natural world, such as honeycombs, which are hexagons, and starfish, which are pentagons. Ask for students to volunteer more examples. The data sheet can serve as a guide in their search for material for their collages.

- Hand out old magazines and newspapers. Instruct your students to search for pictures that show geometry. They should neatly cut out the pictures for their collages.

- Depending on the abilities of your students and their access to the Internet, suggest that they search online for examples of geometry in the natural and man-made world. Instruct them to check with you before downloading or printing any art.

• If your students are familiar with symmetry, suggest that they look for examples of line and rotational symmetry.

• Encourage your students to develop themes for their collages—perhaps pictures of a city or maybe a small town. Again, they should try to include examples of geometry from both the natural and man-made worlds.

• Once your students have begun working on their collages, help them arrange the images neatly and in an attractive manner on poster paper. Suggest that they try different arrangements to achieve balance and clarity. Caution them to use glue or tape neatly.

• Explain to your students that after completing their collages they are to select a title and write a summary identifying the geometry shown in the pictures. If your students have access to computers, encourage them to write their summaries on the computer and print them out.

• Remind your students that at the end of the project they are to share their collages with the class and point out the examples of geometry.

Wrap Up

Have your students show their collages to the class and discuss the examples of geometry their collages contain. Display the collages and summaries.

Extension

Suggest that students look for examples of line and rotational symmetry in their collages.

STUDENT GUIDE 2.1

Geometry All Around Us

Project

Your group is to find examples of geometry. These examples may be from nature, such as a honeycomb, a planet, or a tree trunk. They may be man-made, such as buildings, bridges, or even automobiles. You will then create a collage showing examples of geometry.

Key Steps

1. Make a list of geometric shapes you will search for. Start with lines, angles, squares, rectangles, triangles, and circles.

2. Brainstorm with your group to identify examples of the shapes on your list. The windows of a building may be squares or rectangles. The ripples caused by a pebble thrown into a pond are circles.

3. Divide the task of researching. One member of your group might check old magazines for pictures. Another might check newspapers. Someone else might check reference books. Another member might check the Internet for ideas.

4. Carefully cut out and place your pictures onto poster paper to form a collage. Arrange them in an attractive manner. Neatly glue or tape your pictures to the poster paper.

5. Choose a title for your collage and write a summary explaining the geometry shown in the pictures. Attach your summary to the bottom of your collage.

6. Be ready to share your collage with the class.

Special Tips

- If possible, search for examples on the Internet. Try using the search term *geometry in nature* or *geometry all around us*. Think of other search terms you might use. Before printing any pictures or illustrations, check with your teacher.

- If you think of an example of geometry but cannot find a picture of it, try drawing it. Use markers, crayons, or colored pencils to add details.

To Be Submitted

Your collage and written summary

DATA SHEET 2.2

Geometry Everywhere

Examples of geometry are all around us. They appear in nature and in the man-made world.

Some Examples of Geometry in Man-Made Objects and Structures

Windows: squares, rectangles, circles

Walls, floors, and roofs: parallel and perpendicular lines, angles

Floor tiles: squares

Desks: rectangles

Tables: squares, rectangles, circles

Steering wheels on cars: circles

Football and soccer fields: rectangles

Baseballs, soccer balls, basketballs: spheres

Water towers: cylinders

Bridges: triangles, arcs

Pyramids: triangles

Some Examples of Geometry in Nature

Tree trunks: lines or cylinders

Honeycombs: hexagons

Starfish: pentagons

Worms: cylinders

Snowflakes: hexagons

Snail shells: spirals

Full moon: circle (but actually a sphere)

Animals: symmetry (two eyes, two ears, legs on each side of body)

Ripples in a pond: circles

Look around you to find many more examples.

Planning a Spring Flower Garden

WHETHER YOU ARE PLANTING FLOWERS throughout an entire yard or in just a small plot, planning a flower garden requires several math skills. An understanding of estimation, measurement, geometry, scale, and computation with money are all necessary. This project gives students the opportunity to draw on their skills in these areas to plan a small flower garden. On completion of this project, your students may want to plan and plant real flower gardens for their school or homes.

Goal

Working in groups of three or four, students will be given a budget and a list of flowers. They are to choose plants, calculate the total costs, and make a scale diagram of a flower garden while staying within their budgets. *Suggested time:* three to four class periods.

Skills Covered

1. Computing with money
2. Using data to make a decision
3. Measuring lengths
4. Finding areas
5. Estimating
6. Planning within a budget

7. Making a scale diagram

8. Communicating mathematical ideas and justifying solutions

9. Using technology (if computers or calculators are used)

Special Materials and Equipment

Rulers, yardsticks, string (at least ten feet in length), crayons, colored pencils, and markers. Optional: plant catalogs and garden center circulars, calculators, and computers with Internet access.

Development

- Before beginning this project, consider collecting catalogs from companies that sell flowers, such as mail-order flower companies and local garden centers and nurseries. You might ask colleagues to give you any old catalogs they have. (To protect privacy, be sure to remove any address labels before distributing these catalogs.) Catalogs that contain pictures of plants can help students visualize the flowers they select for their gardens.

- Start the project by asking your students if any of them have flowers outside their homes. It is likely that many do. Discuss how flowers can make a home more attractive, add color to the landscape, and help people feel closer to nature. Explain that for this project they will work in groups to plan and design a flower garden.

- If possible, take your students outside to observe real flower gardens. This excursion will foster their skill in visualization, stimulate their imaginations, and enhance their perception of relationships between plants and landscapes.

- Distribute copies of Student Guide 3.1 and discuss the information it contains. Make certain that your students understand they are to choose a form for their garden, select flowers, arrange the flowers, and keep within a budget of $50. If necessary, discuss what a budget is.

- Explain that each group must select one of two forms for their garden: a square with sides of 2.5 feet or a rectangle with a length of 3 feet and a width of 2 feet. To give students an idea of the size of such gardens, let them measure the dimensions of these figures on the floor. (You may need to push desks apart.) Have them use yardsticks or rulers to measure the lengths of the sides and then use string to mark those lengths.

- You may want to point out that the areas of the two figures are about the same. The area of the square is 6.25 square feet and the area of the rectangle is 6 square feet. Depending on the abilities of your students, you may suggest that they calculate these areas.

- Distribute copies of Data Sheet 3.2: Facts and Prices of Some Common Flowers, which provides descriptions and costs of flowers your students can select for their gardens. The prices are general and the plants listed grow in most areas of the country from early through late spring, but feel free to substitute your own list of plants and prices. Make sure that your students understand the information on the sheet. For example, "size when mature" refers to a plant's height when it is in bloom. If you want to broaden the scope of the project, allow your students also to select plants from catalogs, which usually include color pictures.

• Suggest that your students try to create an attractive garden by choosing different kinds of flowers with different colors. If you do not have catalogs that show the flowers, encourage your students to find pictures of the flowers by consulting reference books or by searching online.

• Emphasize to your students that they must stay within their budgets. Urge them to estimate their costs as they go along.

• Hand out copies of Worksheet 3.3: One-Inch Grid. Students are to design the arrangement of their flowers on the grid. Have extra sheets on hand. Suggest that they plant their flowers about four to six inches apart. Although they can place them in rows, suggest that they might instead create a design that will help their garden to stand out.

• Discuss scale with your students. Because they are working with a one-inch grid, suggest that they choose a scale in which one inch equals one foot. Also suggest that they sketch a rough outline of their garden and lightly mark in pencil where they will place the flowers. They can use letters that represent the names of flowers to show the location of each type of flower on the grid.

• After your students have decided on final arrangements of flowers for their gardens, they should make a final copy on a new grid. Suggest that on this version they use crayons, colored pencils, or markers to designate the location of the flowers. Instruct them to include a color key at the bottom of the grid to identify the types of flowers they used.

• Hand out copies of Worksheet 3.4: Flower Cost Sheet. Explain to your students that they are to list the types of flowers they have chosen for their gardens, the number of each kind of flower, and the total cost of each kind. If necessary, go over the sheet carefully to ensure that they understand how they are to complete it. Calculators can be useful for this part of the project.

• Remind your students to select a spokesperson for their group to share the group's results with the class.

Wrap Up

Display the grids of the finished flower gardens. A spokesperson for each group should explain the group's selection of flowers to the class. Discuss the different arrangements of flowers.

Extensions

Your students could plant real flowers around your school. You might also invite a representative from a local nursery or garden center to speak to the class about planting flowers.

STUDENT GUIDE 3.1

Planning a Spring Flower Garden

Project

Imagine that a local businessperson donated money to your school. The money is to be used to create flower gardens on your school's grounds in time for spring. Your principal would like students to plan the gardens.

Your group will be given a budget of $50. You will also be given a list of flowers and prices and a choice of two sizes for your garden. Your goal is to plan a flower garden without spending more money than your budget allows.

Key Steps

1. Choose either a square or a rectangle for the shape of your flower garden. The square will have sides of 2.5 feet. The rectangle will have a length of 3 feet and a width of 2 feet.

2. Pick different kinds of flowers for your garden. Find pictures of flowers to help you decide what kinds of flowers to choose. You might check flower catalogs or reference books such as encyclopedias. If possible, check sources on the Internet. Search for flowers by their names.

3. Keep track of the costs of the flowers you choose. Estimate your costs as you go along. Do not go over your budget.

4. Sketch a design of your flower garden on one-inch grid paper. Create a scale, such as 1 inch equals 1 foot (12 inches). Place flowers about 4 to 6 inches apart. Mark the spots on the grid where you would plant flowers. Use letters that stand for the names of the flowers. For example, you might use *d* for daffodil or *sg* for snow glories. Try different designs.

5. Once you are pleased with your design, make a final copy of it on a new grid. You might now use colored pencils, crayons, or markers to show where your flowers would be. Be sure to include a color key that shows the flowers you used.

6. Complete Worksheet 3.4. Double-check your math.

7. Choose a spokesperson to share your design with the class.

Special Tips

- Study some real flower gardens. This will give you ideas for planning a flower garden of your own.

- Sketch different plans for how you will arrange your flowers. Shorter or smaller flowers should be placed in front of bigger ones. Otherwise you might not see them.

- You might choose only one kind of flower or many kinds. Think about colors. You might choose flowers with the same color or flowers with different colors. Choose flowers that you believe will look nice in a garden. Use your imagination.

To Be Submitted

A design of your flower bed

Your completed worksheet

DATA SHEET 3.2

Facts and Prices of Some Common Flowers

The following flowers grow in most climates:

Tulips

English Blue Bells

Color: choose from white, pink, and red
Size when mature: 18–20 inches
Bloom: mid to late spring
Price: 5 for $5.99 or 10 for $10.99

Color: blue
Size when mature: 10–14 inches
Bloom: late spring
Price: 3 for $2.85 or 5 for $4.25 or 10 for $7.95

Snow Glories

Color: choose from blue, white, and pink
Size when mature: 4–5 inches
Bloom: early spring
Price: 5 for $3.99 or 10 for $6.99

Facts and Prices of Some
Common Flowers *(Cont'd.)*

Daffodils

Color: choose from yellow and white
Size when mature: 18–20 inches
Bloom: early to mid spring
Price: 3 for $2.99 or 5 for $4.95
or 10 for $8.95

Giant Crocuses

Color: choose from purple, yellow, and white
Size when mature: 4–5 inches
Bloom: late winter to early spring
Price: 5 for $2.99 or 10 for $4.95

Snowdrops

Color: white
Size when mature: 4–6 inches
Bloom: late winter to early spring
Price: 5 for $4.99 or 10 for $7.99 or 20 for $14.99

One-Inch Grid

Flower Cost Sheet

Name of Flower	Number	Cost

Total Cost: _____

Budget _____ − Total Cost = _____

Planning My School Lunch for a Week

FOR MOST STUDENTS, lunch is a time for socializing and gulping some quick bites of food. Few think about lunch until it is lunchtime, and even fewer think of eating a nutritionally balanced lunch. Planning their lunches can help students become aware of healthy food choices, as well as foster their skills in decision making. It can also make an interesting math project.

Goal

Working individually, students are to plan their lunches for a period of one week. They will be given a budget of $14 to spend and are to select foods that will result in healthy, nutritionally balanced lunches. They will create charts to display the foods they chose. *Suggested time:* two class periods.

Skills Covered

1. Estimating and calculating with money
2. Finding an average
3. Using data to make decisions
4. Making a chart to communicate data
5. Using technology (if computers or calculators are used)

Special Materials and Equipment

Rulers, crayons, colored pencils, markers, and 9-by-12-inch drawing paper. Optional: calculators, computers with Internet access and printers.

Development

- Before starting this project, consider asking your school's nurse or your students' health teacher to discuss nutrition with your class, or consider using this project to supplement a unit on nutrition.

- Begin this project by explaining to your students that a well-balanced diet can help them enjoy long, healthy lives. Depending on the nature of your class, you might want to introduce the food pyramid to go along with this activity. Information about the food pyramid and a downloadable miniposter of the pyramid can be found at a Web site maintained by the U.S. Department of Agriculture, http://www.mypyramid.gov.

- Hand out copies of Student Guide 4.1 and review the information it presents with your students. Make sure they understand that they are to work individually and to plan their school lunches by choosing meals from Data Sheet 4.2: Food Choices for School Lunches. The choices are based on the food pyramid. Emphasize that the students are to work with a budget of $14. If necessary, show them how to find the average cost of a day's lunch.

- Distribute copies of Data Sheet 4.2. Discuss the choices on the sheet with your students. Note that they are to select at least one food from each of the groups for each day of the week. This will help them to plan lunches that are nutritionally balanced. Mention that they may choose a snack but are not required to do so.

- Instruct your students to estimate the costs of their lunches as they go along. This will help them stay within their budget.

- Once they have made their choices for lunch, your students are to create a chart displaying their selections. Encourage them to be creative but remind them that they should present their information clearly. They should list each food and its cost, and include a total cost of lunch for each day. Finally, they should include the total cost of their lunches for five days, to show that they stayed within their budget. Suggest that they use colors and illustrations to make their charts attractive.

- Depending on your students' abilities, and on whether they have access to computers, you may prefer that they create their charts using a computer and printer. Most word processing software has capabilities for creating charts and tables.

Wrap Up

Display the charts of student lunches. Discuss which foods were most popular, and stress the importance of nutritionally balanced meals.

Extension

Instruct your students to keep a weekly log of all the foods they eat at each meal. At the end of each week they should review their log and determine if they are maintaining a diet that meets the nutritional requirements of the food pyramid.

STUDENT GUIDE 4.1

Planning My School Lunch for a Week

Project

Imagine that you buy lunch at school each day. You can spend up to $14 each week. If you could choose from many different foods, which ones would you choose? For this project, you will plan your lunches for a week.

Key Steps

1. Choose foods from each of the groups on Data Sheet 4.2.

2. Think about which of the listed foods you like and which you do not like. Think about what you know about making healthy food choices. Choose foods you like that will make a healthy lunch. Estimate your costs as you choose the foods.

3. Start with a weekly budget of $14. Find an average of how much money you will have to spend each day. You do not have to spend the same amount of money for lunch each day. Do not spend more than $14 for the week.

4. Make a chart to show the foods you chose and how much they cost.

Special Tips

- Choose snacks only after you have chosen foods from the other groups.

- A simple chart might contain five boxes. Each box would be for one day of the week. In each box, list the foods for that day. Include the price of each food. Write the total cost of lunch for each day below the box for that day. At the bottom of your chart, calculate the total cost of all your lunches. Subtract this total from $14 to show that you stayed within your budget.

- Be neat when making your chart. Use rulers to make straight lines. Write clearly. Use colors and pictures to make your chart attractive.

To Be Submitted

Your chart

DATA SHEET 4.2

Food Choices for School Lunches

Choose at least one food from each category for lunch each day. You do not have to choose a snack.

Meats and Grains (Bread and Pasta)

Hot dog, $0.95

Chicken nuggets with roll, $1.05

Chicken sandwich, $1.05

Spaghetti with meat sauce, $1.05

Hamburger, $1.25

Tacos, $1.45

Fish nuggets with roll, $1.05

Fish sandwich, $1.05

Macaroni and beef, $1.25

Pepperoni pizza, $1.15

Turkey nuggets with roll, $1.05

Turkey sandwich, $1.05

Fruits

Apple, $0.35

Banana, $0.45

Orange, $0.35

Pear, $0.45

Fruit cup, $0.45

Orange juice (pint), $0.35

Grape juice (pint), $0.35

Apple juice (pint), $0.30

Vegetables

Tossed salad, $0.45

French fries, $0.55

Corn, $0.45

Broccoli, $0.45

Peas, $0.45

Mixed vegetables, $0.45

Carrot sticks, $0.45

Beans, $0.45

Milk and Milk Products

Milk (pint), $0.40

String cheese, $0.40

Yogurt, $0.45

Ice cream (cup), $0.55

Ice cream sandwich, $0.95

Snack Items

Potato chips, $0.35

Pretzels, $0.25

Cookie, $0.25

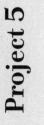

Weather
Observers

BY AN EARLY AGE KIDS are aware of the weather, but they probably do not know how much math can be involved in studying the weather. The weather is a fine subject for a math project in which students observe, analyze, and communicate facts about what is happening outside.

Goal

Working in pairs or groups of three, students will select five cities along with their own city, town, or area and record specific weather conditions for a period of five days. At the end of this period they will organize and compare their data, displaying their findings in graphs, tables, or charts. They will also write a summary of their results. *Suggested time:* two to three class periods (with the possibility of some time being spent outside of class).

Skills Covered

1. Gathering and comparing data
2. Communicating information in the form of graphs, tables, or charts
3. Using writing as a means to express ideas in math
4. Using technology (if computers are used)

Special Materials and Equipment

Rulers, crayons, colored pencils, markers, poster paper, and daily newspapers. Optional: computers with Internet access and printers.

Development

- If another teacher instructs your students in science, you might want to collaborate with him or her on this project. If your students are studying climate or weather, you might use this project to supplement that unit.

- Before starting this project, ask your students how the weather affects them. Answers might include needing to wear heavy clothing in cold weather or light clothing in warm weather, a baseball game being rained out, or school being cancelled because of a snowstorm. If your students are like most, they surely watch the weather report on the night before an approaching winter storm!

- Begin this project by explaining that students will work in pairs or groups of three. They are to record various weather factors in six locations over a five-day period.

- Distribute copies of Student Guide 5.1 and review the information on it with your students. Note that along with their own city, town, or area they are to select five other cities in the United States. You might provide a list of randomly selected cities to choose from; however, encouraging them to choose one city in the Northeast, one in the Southeast, one in the Northwest, another in the Southwest, and another in the heartland can provide a variety of weather conditions. The different groups do not have to select the same places except for their own location. The project will have a broader scope if they choose many different cities.

- Discuss the weather facts they are to record. Depending on the abilities of your students and their background in science, you might suggest that they record other facts as well, such as barometric pressure, dew points, or windchill factors.

- Explain that students are to record data about the weather in the locations they have selected for five days. They may obtain their information from newspapers (most major newspapers contain data about the weather for major cities), TV or radio weather reports, or the Internet. The Web sites of many Internet service providers display weather data, often with search features. An excellent Web site for vast information on weather and forecasts is http://www.weather.com. Data about cities and towns can be obtained through a search by name or ZIP Code.

- Hand out copies of Data Sheet 5.2: Weather Vocabulary, which provides basic weather terms that your students might encounter during this project.

- Explain to your students that after they have compiled their data they are to compare the data using graphs, tables, or charts. Depending on your students' abilities, you may want to limit the data they compare, such as only the temperatures of the locations. Of course you can encourage them to compare as much data in as many ways as they can manage.

- Offer some suggestions for displaying the data. Bar graphs, for example, are a good choice for comparing temperatures among locations and line graphs are a good choice for showing how temperatures rise and fall. A table or chart may be best for displaying data for several weather factors for several locations.

• Suggest that advanced students who have access to computers and printers create graphs, charts, or tables using computer software. You might ask your students' technology instructor to work with them on this.

• Remind your students that they are to write a summary of their data. If possible, encourage them to use a computer for writing and to print their reports. They should express their ideas clearly and edit their writing before handing it in.

Wrap Up

Display your students' graphs, tables, or charts. Discuss their results, especially the differences and similarities in the weather in different parts of the country. Ask them to speculate on what might cause these differences and similarities.

Extension

Instruct students to choose a city in a far northern climate, a city in the middle latitudes, and one in the tropics. Have them record various weather factors for these places over a five-day period. Have them share their results.

STUDENT GUIDE 5.1

Weather Observers

Project

You and your partner or group will record weather facts. You will pick five cities plus your own city, town, or area. You will share your data in a graph, table, or chart. You will also write a summary of your findings.

Key Steps

1. Choose five locations, in addition to your own, to track. These should be major cities. Select cities in different parts of the country. Find the following weather facts for each city:

   Type of day (sunny, partly cloudy, cloudy)

   High and low temperatures

   Precipitation, if any (rain, snow, sleet, hail)

   Wind speed and gusts

   Severe weather, if any

2. Record the weather facts for each location, including your own, for a period of five days.

3. Create graphs, tables, or charts to show your data.

4. Write a report that summarizes your findings. For example, what data were similar? What data were different? Write clearly. Be sure to edit and revise your work. Attach your report to your graph, table, or chart.

Special Tips

- Divide the task of finding information between the group's members. Each person may find information for two or three places.

- Local TV or radio weather reports are good sources for information about your own area. Major newspapers contain information about the weather in many cities across the country. You can also find information about the weather on Internet Web sites.

- See Data Sheet 5.2: Weather Vocabulary for ways to describe the weather.

- Be creative in designing your charts. Use color to highlight your work. You might use symbols to show some of the data. A clear circle can show a sunny day. A half-shaded circle can show a partly cloudy day. A fully shaded circle can show a cloudy day.

- Graphs, tables, charts, and your final summary may be done on a computer.

To Be Submitted

Graphs, tables, or charts

Summary report

DATA SHEET 5.2

Weather Vocabulary

Following are some words that describe weather:

Climate: The average weather of a place over a long period

Cloud: A mass of ice crystals or water droplets in the air

Dew: Moisture that forms on objects near the ground

Dew point: The temperature at which water vapor turns into a liquid

Drizzle: Precipitation of very small droplets of water

Fair: Nice weather

Fog: A cloud that is close to the ground

Front: The area where two weather systems meet

Frost: A thin layer of ice crystals that forms on the ground

Gust: A sudden, brief increase in the speed of the wind

High pressure: An air mass that brings nice weather

Humidity: The amount of water vapor in the air

Hurricane: A very powerful storm that forms over the ocean

Low pressure: An air mass that brings storms

Meteorology: The study of the weather

Partly cloudy: A mix of clouds and sunshine

Precipitation: Moisture that falls from the air as rain (water droplets), snow (ice crystals), sleet (small ice particles), or hail (pellets of ice)

Sunny: Clear weather

Temperature: The amount of heat (or lack of heat) in the air

Tornado: A violently spinning storm

Wind: Moving air

Out of
This World

THE LAUNCHING OF *SPUTNIK I* in 1957 by the Soviet Union began the exploration of space. In the decades since the flight of that first artificial satellite, humans have sent probes throughout our solar system, logged thousands of hours in space, and walked on the moon. Mathematics, of course, plays a major role in the science behind space exploration. Although young students have a long way to go before they master the math skills necessary to send rockets into space, they can use math to make a timeline that celebrates milestones in space exploration.

Goal

Working in pairs or groups of three, students will research and select important events in space exploration. They will use these events to create a timeline and they will explain to the class why the events they chose are in fact milestones. *Suggested time:* two or three class periods.

Skills Covered

1. Using a timeline to represent data
2. Dividing a timeline into fractional units
3. Gathering, sorting, and displaying data
4. Making decisions on the basis of data
5. Using technology (if computers are used)

Special Materials and Equipment

Reference books about space exploration, almanacs, and encyclopedias; rulers; large sheets of drawing or poster paper; markers. Optional: computers with Internet access.

Development

- Discuss space and space exploration with your students. Tell them that space exploration began when the Soviet Union (now Russia) launched a small satellite called *Sputnik I* in 1957. That was the start of the space race between the United States and the Soviet Union. Within the next few years both nations launched numerous probes and sent astronauts and cosmonauts into space. The space race culminated with American astronauts landing on the moon in 1969. It is likely that within the lifetimes of your students, American astronauts will walk on Mars.

- Begin this project by explaining to your students that they will work with a partner or group and create a timeline of space exploration.

- Distribute copies of Student Guide 6.1 and review the information it provides with your students. Tell them that they are to create a timeline from 1950 to the present, and that they are to include the events from Data Sheet 6.2: Some Major Events in Space Exploration, and at least five other major events of space exploration that they research.

- Hand out copies of Data Sheet 6.2, which contains ten events that students are to place on their timelines. Point out that these are only a few of the major events of space exploration and that there are many more for the students to add.

- Encourage your students to consult reference books to find information. If they have access to the Internet, suggest that they check Web sites as well. Searching on terms such as *space exploration* and *space race* will result in numerous useful links. You might also find it helpful to reserve time in your school's library. Speak with the librarian in advance so she can gather books on space exploration.

- Explain to your students that they will need to divide their timelines into equal units. Suggest that they divide them into decades. They might then divide each decade in half, which would give them timelines divided into five-year intervals. Emphasize the importance of dividing their timelines accurately and placing data in the proper place.

- Suggest that students first sketch a draft of their timelines. This will give them a chance to adjust the size of the units. Emphasize that their final copies should be neat as well as accurate.

- Instruct your students to write brief explanations of the events they chose to include on their timelines. (They do not have to write summaries of the events found on Data Sheet 6.2.) The summaries should be written below the timeline and should focus on the importance of the events selected. The summaries should be only a few sentences in length.

- Remind your students that each group should choose a spokesperson to share the group's timeline with the class.

Wrap Up

Have students share their timelines with the class. They should explain their choices and the importance of the events they have chosen.

Extension

Instruct each group to brainstorm about the future of space exploration and predict a milestone event that is yet to come. Have a spokesperson from each group summarize the group's discussion for the class.

STUDENT GUIDE 6.1

Out of This World

Project

You and your partner or group are to create a timeline of space exploration. You will share your results with the class.

Key Steps

1. Read about some of the major events in space exploration on Data Sheet 6.2.

2. Research space exploration in books, almanacs, and encyclopedias or on the Internet.

3. Decide which events to include on your timeline. Include the ten events on Data Sheet 6.2. Include at least five other important events.

4. Set your timeline on the paper horizontally. Start with the year 1950 and go to the present. Divide your timeline into units.

5. Neatly write the dates and events on your timeline. You will need to estimate the location of some events.

6. Below your timeline, write brief explanations of the events you chose. Tell why the events were important.

7. Pick a spokesperson to present your timeline to the class. The spokesperson should explain the events your group chose.

Special Tips

- Divide the tasks of research. Each person might check different reference sources.

- For your timeline, you might make one inch equal to ten years. If you are working on a big piece of paper, you might use two inches for every ten years. You could divide each ten-year period into halves. This would give you five-year periods. Label every ten- or five-year period on your timeline.

To Be Submitted

Your timeline

DATA SHEET 6.2

Some Major Events in Space Exploration

The following events were milestones in space exploration. Include them on your timeline.

1957   The Soviet Union (Russia) launches *Sputnik I*. This was the first artificial satellite.

1958   The United States launches its first satellite, *Explorer I*.

1961   Alan B. Shepard Jr. becomes the first American to travel in space.

1963   Soviet cosmonaut Valentina Tereshkova becomes the first woman to travel in space.

1972   *Apollo 17* is the final flight to land on the Moon.

1976   The unmanned *Viking I* is the first spacecraft to land on Mars.

1981   The *Columbia*, the first U.S. space shuttle, is launched.

1986   The Soviet space station *Mir* is launched.

1990   The Hubble Space Telescope is launched from the space shuttle *Discovery*.

2007   The space shuttle *Endeavor* carries Barbara Morgan, the first teacher to travel in space, to the International Space Station.

Chapter Five

Math and
Social Studies

When in Rome...

MOST STUDENTS TAKE OUR NUMBER SYSTEM for granted. They do not realize that our current number system arose from the work of Hindu and Arabic mathematicians that began more than two thousand years ago. Long before that, many ancient civilizations developed their own number systems. One of the most enduring of these civilizations was that of the ancient Romans. Although Rome fell in 476 A.D., Roman numerals continued to be used throughout Europe for centuries. They still appear on clock faces, in calendars, in copyright dates, in outlines, and as chapter numbers. They provide an excellent means for sharing with your students a glimpse of math in the ancient world.

Goal

Working in pairs or groups of three, students will use Roman numerals to create math problems. They will exchange their problems with other students and solve the problems. *Suggested time:* two class periods.

Skills Covered

1. Using Roman numerals
2. Converting Roman numerals to Arabic numbers
3. Converting Arabic numbers to Roman numerals
4. Computing with basic operations

Special Materials and Equipment

Optional: reference books about the ancient Romans to supplement students' learning.

Development

- This project can support a unit on ancient Western civilizations, particularly the study of ancient Rome. It can help students appreciate the number system of the Romans.

- Begin the project by telling your students that they will work in pairs or groups of three and study Roman numerals. Explain that Roman numerals were the number system used by the ancient Romans. You might mention that the Romans built an empire that stretched from modern-day Great Britain to Asia Minor and controlled the Mediterranean world. If necessary, identify these places on a world map.

- Distribute copies of Student Guide 7.1 and review the information on it with your students. Note that each group is to create a math worksheet based on Roman numerals. They are to write at least four problems, one each for addition, subtraction, multiplication, and division. (Depending on the abilities of your students, you may instruct them to write more than one of each type of problem.)

- Hand out copies of Data Sheet 7.2: The Basics of Roman Numerals, and go over the information it provides. Note that the number system we use today is known as the Arabic system (sometimes referred to as the Hindu-Arabic system). Depending on the nature of your class, you might want to provide additional information. For example, Hindu mathematicians in India were already using an early form of this number system in the second century B.C. By the eighth century A.D. the number system had spread to the Arab world, from which it eventually reached Europe.

- Point out that Arabic numbers are easier to read and use than Roman numerals. For example, the number 8 in Roman numerals is VIII, and the number 28 is XXVIII. Hundreds and thousands are even more complicated. (Although the Romans had a means of writing very large numbers, for this project we suggest that you instruct your students to keep their numbers under a thousand.)

- Make sure that your students understand how to read Roman numerals. Go over the examples on the data sheet. Ask the students to volunteer other examples.

- Mention that the Romans had no symbol for zero. This was a weakness in their number system.

- Remind your students that after they have finished making their worksheets, they must make an answer key for the problems they have created. Also, you might have them make two copies of their worksheets so they can then hand in one copy to you.

- Explain that after creating their worksheets they are to exchange them with another group. Each group is to solve the other group's problems and convert their answers back into Roman numerals. (Rather than having the groups exchange worksheets, you might instead prefer to collect the worksheets, make copies, and then redistribute them to the class, making sure that the groups do not receive their own worksheets. In this way, the students will have the opportunity to see the work of several groups.)

Wrap Up

Discuss your students' impressions of what it is like to work with an ancient number system. How is it easier, or harder, to work with our current Arabic system than to work with Roman numerals?

Extension

Encourage your students to study the number systems of other ancient peoples, such as the Babylonians, Egyptians, Greeks, Chinese, or Mayans.

STUDENT GUIDE 7.1

When in Rome...

Project

You and your partner or group are to create a worksheet with at least four problems written in Roman numerals. You will solve the problems and write the answers in Roman numerals. Then you will exchange worksheets with another group and solve their problems.

Key Steps

1. Study the list of Roman numerals and Arabic numbers on Data Sheet 7.2.

2. Create at least one problem for each of the following operations: addition, subtraction, multiplication, and division. Write your problems in Roman numerals.

3. Make an answer key.

4. Make two copies of your worksheet. Exchange one copy with other students. Hand in the second copy to your teacher.

Special Tips

- When writing your problems, start with Arabic numerals, then convert the problem to Roman numerals.

- To solve a problem written in Roman numerals, first convert the Roman numerals to Arabic numbers. Then solve the problem and convert your answer back to Roman numerals.

To Be Submitted

A copy of your worksheet and your answer key

DATA SHEET 7.2

The Basics of Roman Numerals

According to legend, Romulus and Remus founded the city of Rome in 753 B.C. In time, the Romans came to rule much of the ancient world. They built a great civilization and developed their own number system. The number system we use today is called the Arabic system. This number system was developed in India. It then spread to Arab lands, and from there to Europe.

To understand Roman numerals, follow these rules:

1. Read a Roman numeral from left to right.

2. Roman numerals are formed using some combination of seven capital letters: I = 1, V = 5, X = 10, L = 50, C = 100, D = 500, and M = 1,000.

3. When a symbol of lesser value comes before a symbol of greater value, subtract the lesser value from the greater value. For example, IV = 4 because I = 1 and V = 5 and 5 − 1 = 4.

4. When a symbol of lesser value follows a symbol of greater value, add the lesser value to the greater value. For example, VI = 6 because V = 5 and I = 1 and 5 + 1 = 6.

5. Here are some more examples: XXIV = 24, XLVIII = 48, and XCIX = 99.

The Basics of Roman Numerals *(Cont'd.)*

Roman Numeral		Arabic Numeral	Roman Numeral		Arabic Numeral
I	=	1	XVI	=	16
II	=	2	XVII	=	17
III	=	3	XVIII	=	18
IV	=	4	XIX	=	19
V	=	5	XX	=	20
VI	=	6			
VII	=	7	L	=	50
VIII	=	8			
IX	=	9	C	=	100
X	=	10			
XI	=	11	D	=	500
XII	=	12			
XIII	=	13	M	=	1,000
XIV	=	14			
XV	=	15			

The Mathematics Hall of Fame

FEW STUDENTS GIVE MUCH THOUGHT to the history or development of mathematics. Because they tend to view math in terms of numbers only, they are unaware of the many people who have contributed to the advancement of mathematics. This project offers students an opportunity to learn about some of the men and women who are responsible for our modern understanding and use of math.

Goal

Working in groups of three or four, students will research at least five mathematicians of the past and nominate at least two for a class mathematics hall of fame. Each group will present their nominees to the class and cite reasons for their choices. *Suggested time:* three to four class periods.

Skills Covered

- Researching information about mathematicians
- Evaluating and organizing data
- Making decisions on the basis of the accomplishments of mathematicians
- Communicating ideas about math
- Using technology (if computers are used)

Special Materials and Equipment

Reference books such as encyclopedias and biographies of mathematicians, 3-by-5-inch index cards. Optional: computers with Internet access.

Development

- Ask your students if they are aware of any halls of fame. Some answers might be the National Baseball Hall of Fame and Museum in Cooperstown, New York; the Rock and Roll Hall of Fame in Cleveland, Ohio; and the National Inventors Hall of Fame in Akron, Ohio. Explain that a hall of fame is an institution that honors individuals in a particular field. An individual is inducted into a hall of fame usually in recognition of some great achievement.

- Begin this project by explaining that students will work in groups of three or four. They are to assume that they are members of a committee whose job is to nominate mathematicians to be considered for a class mathematics hall of fame.

- Hand out copies of Student Guide 8.1 and review with your students the information it provides. Explain that they are to research at least five mathematicians from the list offered on Data Sheet 8.2: Candidates for the Mathematics Hall of Fame. Students are to nominate at least two of the individuals they research for induction to the class's mathematics hall of fame. Each group is to make an oral presentation to the class, providing reasons for their nominations.

- Explain to your students that their research should focus on each mathematician's contributions to the field of mathematics. What were this person's great accomplishments? How did he or she help to advance math? Did he or she use math in a new way?

- Because the students will need to consult a variety of reference books, you might wish to schedule time in your school's library for students to conduct research. Speak with your librarian in advance so that he or she can set aside books that might be useful, including encyclopedias, biographies, and books about math. If your students have Internet access, suggest that they research mathematicians online. Depending on the abilities of your students, you may encourage them to continue their research efforts outside of class.

- Hand out copies of Data Sheet 8.2. Mention that not all of the individuals on the data sheet are known primarily as mathematicians; however, each has contributed to mathematics in some way. (Many important mathematicians have been excluded from this list because their major work is high level and not appropriate for students of this age.) Suggest that students choose several mathematicians from the list, do preliminary research on each one to find out if they are interested in learning more about the person, and finally narrow their list down to the ones in whom they are most interested.

- Encourage students to take notes. They should focus their note taking on achievements in math or on applications of math. Emphasize that accomplishments in math are the criterion they are to use in deciding whether a mathematician should be in the class's mathematics hall of fame. Remind your students to write down their sources.

- Make clear that after they have conducted their research, they should choose at least two individuals they will nominate for induction.

- Instruct students to write notes about each nominee on 3-by-5-inch index cards. They should include reasons why the individual should be in the class's mathematics hall of fame.

- Instruct each group to choose a spokesperson to present their nominees to the class. They must provide a strong case for each nominee.

- As your students make their presentations, you may want to list the names of the nominees on the board or project them onto a screen. Include the most important mathematical achievements of each person. After all of the nominees have been presented, have the class vote on five individuals to be inducted into the class's mathematics hall of fame.

Wrap Up

Write on poster paper the names of the mathematicians in your class's mathematics hall of fame and display the poster prominently in the classroom.

Extension

Instruct each group to write a biographical sketch of one of the mathematicians they chose for induction into your class's mathematics hall of fame.

The Mathematics Hall of Fame

Project

Your group is to research mathematicians of the past. You are to nominate at least two for a class mathematics hall of fame. You will present your choices to your class. Be sure to give reasons why you chose these mathematicians.

Key Steps

1. Research at least five of the men and women listed on Data Sheet 8.2. Find the following information for each person:
   - The years they lived
   - Where they were born
   - Their education
   - Their greatest mathematical achievements

2. Divide the task of research. Each person should research different mathematicians. Check reference books and biographies. If possible, check the Internet for information.

3. Discuss the mathematicians that you believe should be in your class's mathematics hall of fame. Base your decisions on their achievements in math. Choose at least two to present to the class.

4. Write the name of each of your choices on a 3-by-5-inch index card. Include general information about these individuals. Also include your reasons for choosing them.

5. Pick a spokesperson to present your choices to the class. Use your index cards to help you remember important ideas. Be sure to state why each mathematician should be in your class's mathematics hall of fame.

Special Tip

- Take accurate notes. Write down your sources. This makes it easy to recheck information if necessary.

To Be Submitted

Your index cards

DATA SHEET 8.2

Candidates for the Mathematics Hall of Fame

Archimedes (287–212 B.C.)

Charles Babbage (1792–1871 A.D.)

Benjamin Banneker (1731–1806 A.D.)

Anders Celsius (1701–1744 A.D.)

René Descartes (1596–1650 A.D.)

Charles L. Dodgson (1832–1898 A.D.)

M. C. Escher (1898–1972 A.D.)

Euclid (about 300 B.C.)

Gabriel Fahrenheit (1686–1736 A.D.)

Pierre de Fermat (1601–1665 A.D.)

Karl Friedrich Gauss (1777–1855 A.D.)

Sophie Germain (1776–1831 A.D.)

Hypatia of Alexandria (370–415 A.D.)

Leonardo da Vinci (1452–1519 A.D.)

Leonardo of Pisa (known as Fibonacci,
    about 1170–1250 A.D.)

Lady Ada Byron Lovelace (1815–1852 A.D.)

John Napier (1550–1617 A.D.)

Blaise Pascal (1623–1662 A.D.)

Pythagoras (about 580–500 B.C.)

Simon Stevin (1548–1620 A.D.)

Thales of Miletus (about 580 B.C.)

The Numbers in a Travel Brochure

WHEN PLANNING A TRIP, most people review travel brochures to find information about their destinations. In addition to estimating the costs of the trip, they may wish to learn about the people, the cities, the history, places to visit, and special events to attend. Much of this information can be described with math.

Goal

Working in pairs or groups of three, students are to choose a country and design a travel brochure. They will use math to highlight the information in their brochures. *Suggested time:* two to three class periods.

Skills Covered

1. Researching mathematical information
2. Analyzing and organizing data
3. Communicating information from a mathematical perspective
4. Measuring length
5. Using technology (if computers are used)

Special Materials and Equipment

Reference books such as atlases, almanacs, and encyclopedias; books about specific countries; rulers; crayons, colored pencils, and markers; 9-by-12-inch drawing paper. Optional: computers with Internet access.

Development

- Collect travel brochures a few days before beginning this project. Perhaps you have some old ones or your colleagues can bring in some from home. Maybe a local travel agency would be willing to donate some. Showing your students actual travel brochures will help them design their own. (Remember to remove any address labels before distributing the brochures to students.)
- Ask your students if they have ever looked through a travel brochure when their family was planning a vacation. Explain that the typical travel brochure contains information about a specific destination, highlighting places to visit and activities for visitors to engage in. Emphasize that most travel brochures contain a lot of math, and give some examples from the sample brochures.
- Start the project by explaining to your students that they are to work in pairs or groups of three. They are to design a travel brochure for a country of their choice.
- Hand out copies of Student Guide 9.1 and review the information provided with your students. Suggest that they select a country they have visited or one they would like to visit.
- Distribute copies of Data Sheet 9.2: Country Highlights. Finding information about the topics on this data sheet will help students create an informative travel brochure. You may wish to encourage them to find information on additional topics as well.
- Encourage your students to use reference books such as atlases, almanacs, and encyclopedias. They may also use books about specific countries. You may find it useful to reserve time in your school's library for research. Inform your librarian in advance so that he or she can assemble the appropriate materials. Depending on the abilities of your students and their access to the Internet, you may suggest that they check for information online.
- Explain to your students that they should pay close attention to math while researching. For example, a country's area (square miles), the elevation of mountains (feet), the length of rivers (miles), the average temperatures (degrees), and the population are all described with numbers. (Costs for travel and lodging are also described with numbers but are not the focus of this project.)
- Hand out copies of Data Sheet 9.3: Directions for Making a Twofold Travel Brochure. Go through the steps shown on the data sheet and make certain your students understand what they are to do. Be sure to point out that they are to divide the paper into fractional parts. Depending on the abilities of your students, you may need to provide assistance. (Note: Using 9-by-12-inch paper makes

measuring easier. You can use smaller or larger paper, but you may need to adjust the measurements for your students.)

• Suggest that your students sketch a rough design of their travel brochure. Explain that this will help them avoid mistakes on their final copy. They should try to visualize where the different topics and information might go. For example, on the front of the brochure they might include the name of the country, an illustration of its flag, and perhaps a picture that shows some special feature. On the left inside page they might include geographical information and a small map. In the middle inside page they might include information about cities. More information can be included on the right inside page and on the back page. There are numerous ways they can design their brochures. Encourage them to be creative, but caution them that a travel brochure should above all be informative and attractive.

• Once your students have completed their research and their rough design, they should make their final brochures. They should be neat, write clearly, and include art. Encourage them to use color to make their brochures appealing.

Wrap Up

Display the travel brochures. Discuss the various designs, with particular emphasis on how numbers are essential to present the information.

Extension

Instruct your students to compare statistics about the country they chose with statistics about their own state. They might be surprised to find that some states, such as New York, California, and Texas, are larger and more populous than many countries.

STUDENT GUIDE 9.1

The Numbers in a Travel Brochure

Project

You and your partner or group are to choose a country and create a travel brochure about it.

Key Steps

1. Choose a country for your travel brochure. This might be a country you have visited, or one that you would like to visit.

2. Find information about your country for the topics listed on Data Sheet 9.2.

3. Check reference books for information. Atlases, almanacs, and encyclopedias are good sources. Books about countries are other sources. If possible, use the Internet to do additional research.

4. Decide which information to include on your travel brochure. To design your brochure, follow the instructions on Data Sheet 9.3.

5. Do a rough copy first. Think about where to place your information. Include written descriptions and pictures. You might also include a small map. Make your brochure attractive.

6. After you have finished your rough copy, create a final copy of your brochure. Write neatly. Draw and color pictures carefully.

Special Tips

- Divide the research so that different people in your group are looking for different information.
- Take accurate notes. Write down your sources. This is helpful if you need to double-check facts.

To Be Submitted

Your final travel brochure

DATA SHEET 9.2

Country Highlights

Find the following information about your country. Include the information in your travel brochure.

1. Name of the country
2. Size of the country in square miles
3. Population
4. Capital city and other major cities and their populations
5. Latitude and longitude of the country
6. Names of the countries that border your country
7. Names of any mountain ranges and the name and elevation of the highest mountain in feet
8. Names of the major rivers and their length in miles
9. Description of the climate (including the average high and low temperatures, and the amount of rainfall in inches)
10. Type of money used in the country
11. Most important language and other major languages
12. Holidays
13. Interesting places to visit
14. Exciting things to do

DATA SHEET 9.3

Directions for Making a Twofold Travel Brochure

1. Use a 9-by-12-inch sheet of paper.

2. Place the paper on your desk so that the 12-inch side runs from left to right.

3. Start near the top of the sheet. From the left edge of your paper measure 4 inches to the right. Mark a point. From this point, measure 4 inches more to the right. Mark another point.

4. Start near the bottom of the sheet, and follow the same steps.

5. Draw a light line to connect the two points that are on the left side of the sheet. Now draw a light line to connect the two points that are on the right side of the sheet.

6. Carefully fold your paper along these lines. Fold along the line on the right side first. Next fold along the line on the left. You should now have the shape of your travel brochure. The folded brochure should be 4 inches wide and 9 inches long. The page facing you should be the cover page. Open the brochure and you should see three equal parts. These parts divide the original 9-by-12-inch sheet into thirds.

7. Make a rough copy of your travel brochure. Think about where you will put the information. For example, the name of the country should be on the cover. You might also put a picture of the country's flag on the cover. Decide what information you will put on the other pages. You may also put information on the back.

8. Create a final copy of your brochure. Write clearly. Draw pictures neatly.

Making a Scale Drawing

U NDERSTANDING SCALE INVOLVES SKILLS that students will use throughout their lives. Practical applications such as interpreting maps, diagrams, blueprints, and floor plans are difficult, if not impossible, without the ability to work with scale. This project gives your students practice with measurement and scale.

Goal

Working in groups of three or four, students will create a scale drawing of their classroom. *Suggested time:* two class periods.

Skills Covered

1. Measuring length
2. Rounding numbers
3. Recognizing the difference between two dimensions (length and width) and three dimensions (length, width, and height)
4. Creating a drawing according to a scale

Special Materials and Equipment

Measuring tapes, yardsticks, and rulers; colored pencils and markers; drawing paper.

Development

- Collect examples of scale drawings to share with your students. Define scale as the relationship of one measurement to another. Discuss that maps, blueprints for houses, floor plans, and certain diagrams are drawn to scale. The scale on a map of a town, for example, might be that 1 inch on the map equals 2 miles in the town.

- Start this project by explaining that students are to work in groups of three or four. They are to make a scale drawing of the classroom.

- Hand out copies of Student Guide 10.1 and review with your students the information it provides. Make sure they understand what a scale drawing is. You may wish to assure them that you do not expect them to be artists for this project; however, you do expect them to work accurately with measurements and scale. Tell them that they are to include desks and tables in their drawings. Depending on their abilities, you may suggest that they include additional items, for example, bookshelves or carts. These will add details and variety to the students' scale drawings. We suggest that unless your students are advanced, they should ignore windows and treat all walls as full walls. They may indicate doors with a blank space.

- Emphasize that the students must take accurate measurements. Make certain they know how to use tape measures and yardsticks. Note that after they take the measurements they should round them to the nearest foot or half-foot. Rounding to inches might result in units that will make their scale drawings overly complicated. If necessary, review rounding with them.

- We suggest that in order to maintain an orderly procedure of measurement you have different groups measure different parts of the classroom at the same time. This reduces logistical logjams.

- Explain to your students that their drawings should be two-dimensional, focusing on length and width. Tell them to imagine being above the classroom and looking down on it. They should not try to draw objects in three dimensions. If necessary, discuss the difference between two dimensions (length and width) and three dimensions (length, width, and height).

- Instruct your students to make a rough sketch of the classroom on drawing paper first. This will help them to see the relationships between furniture and other objects. Depending on your students' abilities, you may prefer to limit the amount of detail in their drawings. For example, if they have pushed their desks together to work in groups, treat each set of desks as a single object. This is easier than treating each desk individually. Tell your students to consider the chairs a part of the desks as well.

- Distribute copies of Data Sheet 10.2: How to Make a Scale Drawing of Your Classroom, and Worksheet 10.3: Half-Inch Grid. Have extra copies of the grid available. Go over the information on the data sheet with your students. Explain that they are to create their scale drawings on the grid. Depending on the size of your classroom, choose an appropriate scale for your students. For most classrooms, "$\frac{1}{2}$ inch equals 2 feet" or "$\frac{1}{2}$ inch equals 3 feet" will work well. The students should make a rough copy first. Only after they are sure of their measurements should they make a final copy. You may find it necessary to monitor your students closely as they follow these directions. Provide guidance as needed.

- After your students have created their scale drawings, they should label the furniture and other major items in the room. They should include the dimensions for objects, and note the scale on the bottom of their drawings.

Wrap Up

Display the students' scale drawings. Discuss similarities and differences in the drawings that may have arisen from the inclusion of different classroom objects.

Extension

Encourage students to do a scale drawing of a section of the classroom. This will, of course, require an entirely different scale.

STUDENT GUIDE 10.1

Making a Scale Drawing

Project

Your group is to make a scale drawing of your classroom.

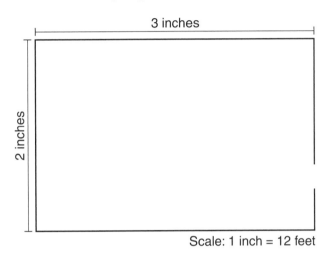

3 inches

2 inches

Scale: 1 inch = 12 feet

Key Steps

1. Decide how much detail you want to include in your drawing.

2. Follow the instructions on Data Sheet 10.2 to create a scale drawing of your classroom.

3. Use Worksheet 10.3 for your drawing. Make a rough copy first. Write the rounded measurements in their proper places on your sketch. Make sure your scale and the objects on your drawing are accurate.

4. Make a final copy of your scale drawing. Use color to make your drawing attactive. Be sure to write your scale on the bottom of your drawing.

Special Tips

- Divide the task of measuring the room among your group's members.

- Use a measuring tape or yardstick to find the dimensions of your classroom. Start at the end of one wall and measure to the other end. Do this for each of the walls.

- As you measure, make a rough sketch of your classroom.

- Include desks and tables in your drawing. You may also include other things such as bookcases or computer stands. Measure the length and width of each object. Do not measure the height.

To Be Submitted

Your scale drawing

DATA SHEET 10.2

How to Make a Scale Drawing of Your Classroom

1. Measure the lengths of the walls.

2. Measure the length and width of the objects you will include in your drawing. (Do not measure their height.)

3. Round your measurements to the nearest foot or half-foot (6 inches).

4. Use the scale your teacher suggests for your drawing.

5. Make a rough copy of your scale drawing first. Count out the units on your grid to find where each object should be placed. You may need to estimate for some objects.

6. When you feel your rough copy is correct, draw a final copy.

7. Include dimensions for objects.

8. Be sure to write your scale at the bottom of your drawing.

Name _____ Date _____

Half-Inch Grid

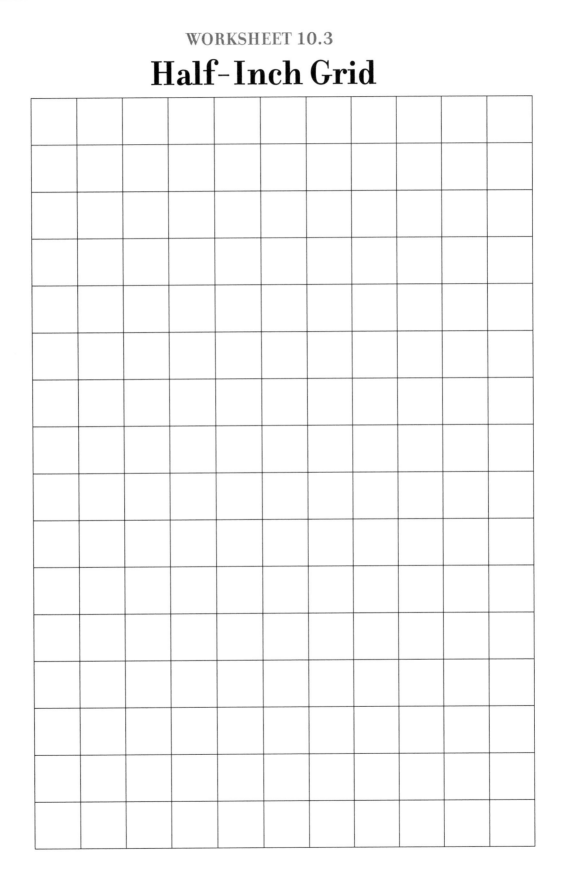

Favorites

EVERYONE HAS HIS OR HER FAVORITES, whether movies, books, TV shows, singers, pets, political candidates, flavors of ice cream, or whatever. For this project, students survey their classmates to find out their favorites in a variety of categories.

Goal

Working in groups of three or four, students will survey their classmates and identify their favorites in a specific category. They will display the results in a bar graph, which they will present to the class. *Suggested time:* two to three class periods.

Skills Covered

1. Gathering data via a survey
2. Constructing frequency tables and determining the frequency of responses
3. Using a bar graph to represent data
4. Communicating mathematical ideas
5. Using technology in problem solving (if computers are used)

Special Materials and Equipment

Rulers, markers, colored pencils, crayons, and 9-by-12-inch drawing paper. Optional: computers and printers for creating bar graphs.

Development

- Discuss surveys with your students. Explain that surveys are a way for researchers to gather information. For example, surveys may be used to find out people's opinions on issues, politicians, and products, or just about anything on which the researchers wish to seek opinions.

- Begin this project by telling your students that they will be working in groups of three or four. They will survey their classmates on a topic, organize their data, and display their data in a bar graph.

- Distribute copies of Student Guide 11.1 and review with your students the information it contains. Make certain they understand that they are to conduct the survey, record their results in a frequency table, and then create a graph that shows their results. Tell them that after picking a topic for their survey, they should provide five possible choices of favorites from which their respondents may pick. Caution them that providing too many choices may result in a lot of data, which may be difficult to show in a graph. Offer them an example such as the following: the topic is ice cream and the five choices of favorites are chocolate, vanilla, strawberry, pistachio, and other.

- Hand out copies of Data Sheet 11.2: Survey Topics. Review the information with your students. Point out that the data sheet contains categories or topics they may choose for their survey. You may also encourage them to pick other topics that are not on the sheet; however, do not permit different groups to select the same topics. If they do, their frequency tables and graphs may be the same.

- Distribute copies of Data Sheet 11.3: How to Make a Frequency Table and discuss the information provided. Explain to your students that before they can make a bar graph, they must first gather data and make a frequency table. Discuss the sample frequency table provided on the data sheet and the steps for making it.

- After your students have selected their topics and the favorite choices for those topics, the members of each group should proceed in an orderly fashion to interview the members of other groups about their favorites. To speed things along, provide a time limit of five minutes for each interview. Suggest that after one group interviews another group, the group that was interviewed should then interview the group that interviewed them. Thus, after Group A interviews Group B, Group B then interviews Group A. This approach reduces the amount of movement in the classroom. Each group should interview every other group. Emphasize that the data each group obtains from the rest of the class should be combined, tallied on the group's frequency table, and displayed in one graph.

- Students should create their graphs on 9-by-12-inch paper (unless they are using a computer). If necessary, offer them guidelines for creating their graphs. For example, they should determine whether the bars in their graph will extend vertically or horizontally. Note that each choice of favorite should be represented with its own bar, and that the lengths of the bars will depend on the frequency. Caution your students to choose an appropriate scale. For example, they might use a $\frac{1}{4}$-inch or $\frac{1}{2}$-inch for each tally. The scale depends, of course, on the number of responses for each choice. The group members should choose a scale that will allow them to draw bars of the appropriate length. Remind them to title their graphs and label their data. Depending on the abilities of your students and the accessibility of computers, you might encourage them to enter their data into a computer program and generate a graph using software such as Microsoft Excel.

Wrap Up

Have students show their graphs to the class. Displaying the graphs will reveal an assortment of class favorites.

Extension

Have your groups survey students in other classes. Instruct them to draw new graphs using this new data. Note how the results found in your class compare to the results of the new sample.

Name _____   Date _____

STUDENT GUIDE 11.1

Favorites

Project

Your group is to find favorite things of your classmates. You will choose a topic. Then you will survey your classmates. You will create a frequency table and a bar graph of your results.

Key Steps

1. Choose a topic that interests you for your survey. You may choose a topic from Data Sheet 11.2 or a topic of your own.

2. Offer about five choices for favorites. For example, for the topic *favorite fruits* you might offer the choice of apples, bananas, pears, oranges, or peaches. You might also offer "other" as a choice.

3. Make a frequency table for recording your data (see Data Sheet 11.3).

4. Create a bar graph using the data from your frequency table. Use an accurate scale. For example, you might use units of $\frac{1}{4}$ or $\frac{1}{2}$ inch to show each tally.

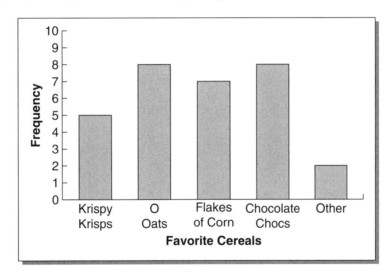

Special Tips

- Start your survey by asking your classmates this question: Which of the following is your favorite?

- Use colored pencils, crayons, or markers to make your graph attractive. You may also use a computer to create the graph. Be sure that all lines are straight, all bars are labeled, and all data are shown. Remember to title your bar graph.

To Be Submitted

Frequency table and bar graph

DATA SHEET 11.2

Survey Topics

A survey asks a question, or questions, of people. Surveys are a means of gathering information. Choose one of the following topics for your survey, or choose a topic of your own. Find out your classmates' favorites for your topic.

Movies	Sports
TV shows	Foods
Pets	Ice cream flavors
Novels	Snacks
Singers or singing groups	Colors
Harry Potter books	After-school activities
School subjects	Games

Some Survey Vocabulary

Bar graph: a type of graph in which the lengths of bars show the data

Data: information gathered about people or things

Frequency: the number of times an answer is given

Frequency table: a table that organizes the results of a tally

Sample: the people who are surveyed

Tally: the total number of answers to a question

DATA SHEET 11.3

How to Make a Frequency Table

A frequency table is useful for organizing data. Following is an example of a frequency table showing favorite cereals. It is based on a survey of 30 students.

Favorite Cereals

Responses	Tally	Frequency
Krispy Krisps	ⅢⅢ	5
O Oats	ⅢⅢ |||	8
Flakes of Corn	ⅢⅢ ||	7
Chocolate Chocs	ⅢⅢ |||	8
Other	||	2

Here are some tips for making a frequency table:

1. Make a table with three columns.

2. In the first column, write the answers to your survey.

3. In the second column, write the number of people who chose each answer. Make a tally mark each time an answer is given.

4. In the third column, write the total number of tally marks for each answer.

5. The total number of tally marks for all answers should equal the number of people you surveyed.

Scavenger Hunt for Math in Our Lives

MATHEMATICS IS WOVEN into all areas of our lives. Examples of math are so common that they are easy to overlook. We seldom give a second thought to the math behind our daily routines. This project gives students a chance to find math just about everywhere. It should help them to gain a greater understanding and appreciation of the math in their lives.

Goal

Working in pairs or groups of three, students will generate a list of examples of how math is used in their lives. They will create a poster highlighting the examples they found and provide details. *Suggested time:* two class periods.

Skills Covered

1. Identifying the use of numbers and mathematics in various real-life situations
2. Connecting math to everyday events and situations
3. Communicating about math

Special Materials and Equipment

Reference books such as atlases and almanacs, old magazines and newspapers, rulers, crayons, markers, and poster paper.

Development

- Before beginning this project, collect old magazines and newspapers, which can help your students find examples of math in a variety of instances. Perhaps colleagues or your school's librarian can donate some. (Remember to remove any address labels before distributing such publications to your students.)
- Ask your students if they have ever watched a sporting event, checked a watch or clock for the time, or paid for an item with money. Explain that math is a part of each of these examples, as well as of countless other objects and activities in our everyday lives.
- Begin this project by explaining to your students that they will work with a partner or in a group of three to generate a list of at least ten examples of how math is used in everyday life. They are to create a poster showing these examples.
- Hand out copies of Student Guide 12.1 and review the information it provides with your students. Tell them that they are to seek examples of math in all areas of their lives, and these examples must be specific. For instance, they cannot simply say that time is based on math. They must explain how this is so. One explanation might be that time is based on a twenty-four-hour day, and an hour can be divided into sixty minutes, which in turn can be divided into sixty seconds. Accept explanations in accordance with the abilities of your students.
- Encourage your students to brainstorm to find examples and ideas. They can probably find many ideas by reflecting on their own experiences. Suggest that in addition to brainstorming they consult reference books and textbooks, especially on math, science, and social studies, for ideas. Expand their research materials by handing out copies of magazines and newspapers.
- Hand out copies of Data Sheet 12.2: Math in Many Places. Point out that the data sheet contains general topics. Students should discuss these topics in their search for examples of math in life.
- Explain that once they have generated their ideas, they are to create a poster that highlights at least ten examples of ways math is used in our lives. They should write out each example and explain how math applies to it.
- If necessary, guide your students through the process of planning and making their posters. For example, they must measure spaces for lines, draw lines lightly, and write neatly and clearly.

Wrap Up

Display the posters. Discuss the examples of math your students found. Especially point out the most unusual instances. The incredible scope of mathematics should become apparent to your students.

Extension

Ask your students to generate additional examples of math according to specific topics, for example, the human body, a rain forest, or school.

STUDENT GUIDE 12.1

Scavenger Hunt for Math in Our Lives

Project

You and your partner or group are to find examples of math in your lives. You should find at least ten examples. You will then create a poster showing your examples.

Key Steps

1. Brainstorm ideas about how math is used in the things you do.
2. Find examples of math for the topics listed on Data Sheet 12.2.
3. Choose the ten examples that you think are most important or interesting. Create a poster that shows and describes them.

Special Tips

- Check different sources for ideas, such as almanacs and atlases. You might include some of your textbooks. You might also check magazines and newspapers.
- Follow these tips to make your chart:
  - Use a ruler to measure spaces.
  - Draw lines lightly in pencil.
  - Write and explain each example of math on its own line.
  - You may want to draw illustrations to decorate your poster.
  - Remember to title your poster.

To Be Submitted

Your poster

DATA SHEET 12.2

Math in Many Places

You can find many examples of math in life. Here are some places to look. Write at least one idea for each topic.

Time: _____

Sports and games: _____

Science: _____

Nature: _____

Geography: _____

Buildings and architecture: _____

Hobbies: _____

Travel: _____

Shopping: _____

Food and cooking: _____

Computers: _____

The Earth: _____

Chapter Six

Math and Language Arts

A Class Math Newsletter

WRITING, PRODUCING, AND PUBLISHING a class newsletter about math offers students a chance to bring together a variety of skills in a project that will add a new dimension to your math class. Not only is it easy to produce your class's newsletter with a photocopier, but with a computer and Internet access you can also post the newsletter for the world to see. Creating a class math newsletter enables your students to showcase their knowledge, interests, and progress in math.

Goal

Working in groups of three to five, students will create and produce a class newsletter devoted to math. *Suggested time:* four to five class periods; however, this time may be divided over several partial class periods. Students may also work outside of class.

Skills Covered

1. Various math skills depending on the topics in the newsletter
2. Communicating ideas about math through writing and illustrating
3. Using technology (if a computer is used)

Special Materials and Equipment

Scissors, tape, glue, rulers, staplers, felt-tip pens, markers, copy paper, and photocopier. Optional: computers and printers, clip art, and Internet access for posting the newsletter online.

Development

- Because posting your class's monthly math newsletter online is an option, you might want to work with your school's technology instructor on this project. You might also consider working with your students' art teacher, who can be helpful with design and illustrations.

- Before beginning this project, set guidelines for yourself and your students. If this is your first experience producing a class math newsletter, we suggest that you limit its size and scope. Two pages (one sheet of paper with material on both sides) or four pages (two sheets with material on both sides) will provide enough space for your students to write short articles and will be small enough for you to manage. As you gain experience writing and producing newsletters, you may decide to increase their size.

- You also need to decide what content to include in the newsletter. All material should of course focus on math. You might encourage your students to write articles about math, create puzzles (see Project 29), or write challenge problems. Some students might like to create a short math comic strip or cartoon (see Project 21) or a math poem (see Project 15). The newsletter may address a broad range of math topics, or it may concentrate on specific topics, such as basic operations, fractions and decimals, or geometry. Maybe you would prefer your students to address topics in the unit they are currently studying.

- Start the project by explaining to your students that they will work in groups, with all groups contributing to the production of a class newsletter. Explain that a typical newsletter contains articles on a particular subject aimed at a specific audience. In this case, students are to create a class math newsletter for other students. Upon conclusion of the project, copies of the newsletter will be distributed to students.

- If you have copies of math newsletters from other classes, hand them out so that your students can examine them. Most of your students have probably never been involved in creating a class publication.

- You may want to brainstorm possible names for your class's newsletter. Having students suggest names gets them involved from the start and helps give them ownership of the project.

- Hand out copies of Student Guide 13.1 and review the information it contains with your students. Emphasize that each group will be responsible for a part of the newsletter. Everyone will contribute to the whole.

- Organize the focus of your groups. For example, one group may be responsible for writing articles, another group may write challenging brainteasers, another may concentrate on creating art, another may make graphs or charts, and yet another may write a column of math tips. Consider matching group assignments with the interests of your students. Those students who enjoy writing may prefer to write articles while those who like to draw may prefer doing the artwork for the newsletter. Students who love math challenges might like to create puzzles.

- Hand out copies of Data Sheet 13.2: Guidelines for Creating a Class Math Newsletter, which contains several ideas that can be developed into material for your class's newsletter, as well as some tips for writing. (You may also want to hand out copies of Math and the Writing Process, found in Chapter Two of this book. The information provided there may help your students as they write material for the newsletter.)

• Although your students may write articles for the newsletter in long hand, encourage them to write their articles on the computer, if possible. Writing on the computer serves several ends: saving their articles in a word processing file will aid the revision process, printed text makes for a very attractive newsletter, and electronic files will allow you to post the newsletter on a school Web site, which will delight students, parents, and administrators.

• Your students can illustrate their newsletter. Dark line illustrations may be drawn on separate sheets of paper, then cut out and pasted onto the pages of the newsletter. We suggest that you do not permit students to draw directly on a finished page. Mistakes in art may mean having to redo the whole page. (Although white correction fluid can rectify a host of errors, every attempt should be made to keep final copies free of mistakes.) If you have access to a color photocopier, you may permit your students to use color in their illustrations; keep in mind, however, that some colors reproduce better than others, and color copies can be costly.

• Note that clip art, which is available with many software programs as well as online, is another source of illustrations. Be sure that any clip art that students use is copyright free.

• Because your groups will be involved with different activities while working on the newsletter, you will need to monitor their progress closely. Set deadlines for when work should be done, and remind students frequently of their deadlines.

• Once the groups have finished their work, they should carefully proofread their writing and check their math facts. You should also proofread and double-check their work to ensure accuracy and to make certain that all errors have been caught. It is too late to make corrections once copies of the newsletter have been printed and distributed.

• To find an attractive design for the newsletter, experiment with "dummy" layouts. Simply place copies of the finished materials—the articles, puzzles, and art, for example—on a sheet of white paper that will serve as a page of the newsletter. Include headlines and titles. Arrange and rearrange the material until you find a layout that is attractive and easy to read. You might have students help you with this. After you have decided on a final format, tape or glue the materials to the page. Make one photocopy of each finished page, and check to make sure that no stray lines or shadows appear where the articles or art were pasted or taped onto the page. If errant lines are visible, hide them with correction fluid. Of course if your students have written their articles on the computer, you can design the newsletter using word processing or publishing software.

• Photocopy the newsletter. Copying on both sides of the sheet not only saves paper but results in a high-quality publication. Make enough copies for each of your students, as well as copies for administrators and for displays around the school. If the newsletter is longer than one sheet of paper, staple the pages together. If it is stored in a word processing file, post it on your school's Web site.

Wrap Up

Distribute copies of the newsletter. Encourage your students to read and respond to the work of their classmates.

Extension

Make the production of a class newsletter a continuing part of your math program. You might publish a new newsletter each marking period.

STUDENT GUIDE 13.1

A Class Math Newsletter

Project

Your class is to write and publish a math newsletter. You will be divided into groups. Each group will work on a different part of the newsletter. Once the newsletter is finished, copies will be made and handed out.

Key Steps

1. Decide what material your group will contribute to the newsletter. You may write articles, create math puzzles, create art, or write something else that has to do with math. See Data Sheet 13.2 for some ideas.

2. Edit and revise your writing.

3. Recheck the math facts.

4. If you write math challenge problems or create puzzles, include an answer key.

5. Hand in your finished material to your teacher.

Special Tips

- Brainstorm ideas for the newsletter before you start writing. Remember that all material should be about math.

- Divide the work of your group. For example, some group members might write articles. One member might edit and proofread the articles. Another might double-check the math problems.

- Research topics if necessary. Books about math, including your math textbook, are good sources.

- Manage your time. Keep track of your progress. Be sure to meet your deadlines.

- Any drawings should be done in dark, clean lines. Do not use shading. Sometimes shading does not copy well. Check with your teacher before using color on any drawings. Also check with your teacher if you intend to use any clip art.

To Be Submitted

Your group's work for the newsletter

DATA SHEET 13.2

Guidelines for Creating a Class Math Newsletter

Following are some ideas for a math newsletter:

- Articles about math
- Articles about math students of the month
- Math homework hints
- Information about math contests
- Information about the school's math club
- Math brainteasers or puzzles
- Math cartoons
- Math trivia
- Biographical sketches of mathematicians

Tips for Writing About Math

1. Choose an interesting idea to write about.
2. Gather information.
3. Use an opening, body, and closing in your writing.
4. Support your main ideas with details.
5. Double-check your math facts.
6. Edit, revise, and proofread your writing.

Family Matters and Math

MATHEMATICS PLAYS a part in many professions, occupations, and activities. As students become aware of the role of math in daily routines, they gain a greater appreciation of math. As they complete this project, they will learn about the importance of math through members of their families.

Goal

Working individually, students will interview a family member about the importance of math in that person's daily routines. They will then write an article based on their interview. *Suggested time:* two class periods, with some time spent outside of class to conduct the interviews.

Skills Covered

1. Various math skills depending on the content of students' articles
2. Communicating ideas about math through writing
3. Using technology (if computers are used)

Special Materials and Equipment

Optional: pads for taking notes during interviews, computers and printers for writing articles.

Development

- Explain to your students that most people use math in some way every day. They might use math in their job, when budgeting their shopping, or when paying bills and balancing their checkbook. Ask your students to volunteer examples of how some of their family members use math.
- Begin this project by explaining to your students that they are to interview a member of their family—a parent, grandparent, older brother or sister, aunt or uncle—to find out how this person uses math in his or her job or at home. Make sure the students understand that they are to interview only a family member. They should not interview a neighbor or friend.
- Distribute copies of Student Guide 14.1. Review with your students the information it provides and make certain they understand what they are to do. You might need to explain the interviewing process.
- Hand out copies of Data Sheet 14.2: Interview Tips. Discuss the tips with your students, especially the suggestions for asking open-ended questions that require an explanation and not simply a yes or no answer. Remind them to take notes, but advise them not to try to write down everything. They should instead focus on the most important information.
- Depending on your students' abilities, you may want to discuss quoting the people they interview. Explain that any exact statements must be set in quotation marks and identified as the words of the speaker.
- Explain to your students that after they have finished their interviews they should organize their notes and write their articles. Encourage them to use the following structure: opening, body, and closing. Remind them to support their main ideas with details, and to edit, revise, and proofread their writing.
- Depending on the abilities of your students and their access to computers, you might suggest that they write their articles on the computer.

Wrap Up

Display your students' articles. Use them as a springboard for discussion of the many ways people use math in their everyday lives.

Extension

Invite a family member whose math skills are essential to his or her job—such as an engineer, banker, architect, surveyor, actuary, or landscaper—to speak to the class about how he or she uses math.

STUDENT GUIDE 14.1

Family Matters and Math

Project

You are to interview a member of your family to find out how he or she uses math at a job or at home. After the interview, you will write an article about what you learned.

Key Steps

1. Think about whom you will interview. Make sure it is someone in your family, such as a parent, grandparent, older brother or sister, or aunt or uncle. Do not interview a friend or neighbor. Do not interview anyone without your parent's or guardian's permission.

2. Before the interview, write down some questions to ask.

3. Set up a time for your interview. You may meet in person or you may do the interview by phone or e-mail.

4. During the interview, ask the questions you wrote down before the interview. Take careful notes.

5. After the interview, organize your information.

6. Write your article. Be sure it has an opening, body, and closing. Support your main ideas with details. Edit, revise, and proofread your writing.

Special Tips

- Be sure to have paper and two pens ready for your interview. (Use the second pen if the first one runs out of ink.)

- If possible, write your article on a computer.

To Be Submitted

Your article

DATA SHEET 14.2

Interview Tips

In an interview, a writer asks another person questions about a topic. Writers can find out much information through an interview. Following are some tips.

1. Ask questions that have detailed answers. Such questions will give you more information. Do not ask questions that can be answered with yes or no. For example, do not ask, "Is math important to your job?" Instead ask, "How is math important to your job?" The first question can be answered with yes. The second must be answered with details.

2. Sometimes the answer to a question will lead to another question. Be alert to such questions and be sure to ask them. This is how you find out a lot of information.

3. Do not try to write down everything the person says. Write down the most important facts.

4. If you do not understand an answer, ask the person to explain.

5. For the most important facts, write down the person's exact words. Remember that if you use his or her exact words in your article, you must put quotation marks around them.

6. Once the interview is finished, thank the person. Remember, this person gave up his or her time to help you.

Writing Poetry About Math

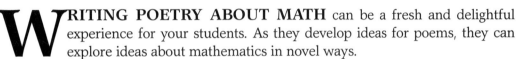

WRITING POETRY ABOUT MATH can be a fresh and delightful experience for your students. As they develop ideas for poems, they can explore ideas about mathematics in novel ways.

Goal

Working individually or in pairs, students will write at least one poem about math. They will be given a choice of writing a haiku, a limerick, or a concrete poem. *Suggested time:* two class periods.

Skills Covered

1. Various math skills depending on the content of students' poems
2. Writing as a means of expressing ideas about math
3. Using technology (if computers are used)

Special Materials and Equipment

Dictionaries and thesauruses, and anthologies of poetry from which you can share examples of poems with your students. Optional: rhyming dictionaries and computers with Internet access.

Development

• There are many forms of poetry. This project focuses on haikus, limericks, and concrete poems, which are suitable for young students. You may wish to expand the project to include other kinds of poetry as well.

- Because many students are uneasy with writing poetry, you might allow them to work in pairs for this project. Students who are excited about poetry, however, should be encouraged to work alone. Sharing examples of poems with your students is helpful. Your school library undoubtedly has anthologies of poetry for students, or your might check online for samples of poems. A simple search on the form of poetry you are looking for, such as haiku, will yield numerous Web sites and examples. Caution: before you direct students to any poetry Web sites, check to make certain that these sites do not contain any poems that have inappropriate content. We have also found the following books to be fine resources for teaching poetry to students:

> *Rose, Where Did You Get That Red?* by Kenneth Koch (1990)
>
> *Tiger Lilies, Toadstools, and Thunderbolts: Engaging K–8 Students with Poetry* by Iris McClellan Tiedt (2002)
>
> *The Haiku Handbook: Write, Share, and Teach Haiku* by William J. Higginson (1997)
>
> *A Poke in the I: A Collection of Concrete Poetry* by Paul B. Janeczko (2001)

- Start this project by explaining to your students that they will work individually or with a partner. They are to write at least one poem about math. They may write about a specific topic in math, for example, a geometric concept or figure, an operation, math homework, the importance of math, or their feelings about math. Encourage them to find topics that are personally meaningful to them. This will help them to write stronger poems.
- Distribute copies of Student Guide 15.1 and review the information provided with your students. You may encourage them to write more than one poem if they wish. If they do write more than one, suggest that they write different types of poems.
- Hand out copies of Data Sheet 15.2: Three Types of Poems, and discuss the poems on the sheet.
- Explain that *haiku* is a form of Japanese poetry. Although the original purpose of haiku was to celebrate or present an observation of nature, modern haikus are written on a broad range of subjects. Emphasize the special form of haikus: they have three lines with a specific syllabic count—five syllables in the first line, seven in the second, and five in the third. If necessary, review syllables with your students and provide them with some examples. Instruct them to consult a dictionary if they are not certain of the number of syllables in a word. Point out the example of haiku on the data sheet. If you have other examples, share these as well. Perhaps write a haiku on the board or overhead screen as a class exercise.
- Explain that *limericks* are a humorous, structured form of poetry. They were popularized by Edward Lear, an English painter and humorist of the nineteenth century. Limericks have a specific cadence and rhyming pattern. Lines one, two, and five, called a *triplet*, rhyme. Lines two and four, called a *doublet*, also rhyme. Read the sample limerick on the data sheet so your students can hear its rhythm and rhyme. Providing other examples will help them appreciate and understand this unique poetry form. You might want to do a class example on the board or overhead screen.

- Explain that *concrete poems*, also known as shape poems or visual poems, take the form of their subject. Point out the example on the data sheet, which is written in the shape of a rectangle. A poem about addition might be in the shape of a plus sign (+) while a poem about multiplication might be in the form of an X. Concrete poems may or may not rhyme, but they are always in the form of their subject. Offer other examples and perhaps create an example together.
- If you wish, share with your students other examples of poetry, both non-rhyming and rhyming. Keep in mind that rhyming poems can be difficult for some students.
- If you have a rhyming dictionary available, discuss its use with your students. You might also explain that they can create rhyming word lists to help them write poetry with rhyme. They can generate such word lists individually or work with a partner. You might also make the creation of rhyming word lists a class exercise. Following are some examples:

day, bay, hay, hey, say, weigh, tray, hooray. . . .

blue, new, knew, dew, you, few, kangaroo, too, to, two. . . .

snow, ho, low, go, no, tow, throw, blow, crow, hello, so, sew. . . .

- Depending on the abilities of your students, distribute copies of Data Sheet 15.3: Tips for Poets. Explain that writers and poets often use alliteration and figures of speech to express their ideas with more clarity and power. Go over the examples provided on the data sheet and ask your students to volunteer more examples. Encourage them to use alliteration and figures of speech in their own writing.
- Suggest that your students use dictionaries and thesauruses to find words that will help them express their ideas. If necessary, review the use of these references with your students. Especially note the differences between a dictionary and a thesaurus. A dictionary contains words alphabetically arranged and their meanings. The words in a dictionary are also broken into syllables and have a pronunciation key. Many students mistakenly believe that a thesaurus is a type of dictionary. Point out that a thesaurus is primarily a book of synonyms, although some thesauruses also contain antonyms.

Wrap Up

Organize a poetry reading session and ask your students to read their poems to the class. Display their math poems on a bulletin board.

Extensions

Encourage your students to write more poems about math and publish them in a class math poetry anthology.

You might also organize a math poetry evening. Invite parents, teachers, and administrators to listen to your students read their math poems.

Writing Poetry About Math

Project

Working alone or with a partner, you are to write a poem about math.

Key Steps

1. Read examples of poems. Some poems have special forms. Check Data Sheet 15.2 for an example of a haiku, a limerick, and a concrete poem. Choose one of these forms for your poem.

2. Think of a topic in math. How might you write about this topic in a poem?

3. Write a rough draft of your poem. Revise and rewrite it until you are satisfied with it.

Special Tips

- If you plan to write a poem with rhyme, you might want to use a rhyming dictionary. You might also create a rhyming word list.

- Try to find the best words to express your ideas. Use a dictionary or thesaurus to help you find the right words. You can also use a dictionary to find the number of syllables in a word.

- If your poem has a special form, you must follow this form. You must count syllables for the lines in a haiku. You must follow the rhyme pattern and rhythm of a limerick. The words in a concrete poem must take the shape of the poem's subject.

To Be Submitted

Your finished poem

DATA SHEET 15.2

Three Types of Poems

Following are three kinds of poems. Each has a very special form.

- *Haiku* is a type of Japanese poetry. It is written in three lines. The first line has five syllables. The second line has seven syllables. The third line has five syllables. Here is an example of haiku:

> Math is wonderful.
> It's my favorite subject.
> I like learning math.

- A *limerick* is a silly poem. It has five lines and a special rhyme pattern. The first, second, and fifth lines rhyme. The third and fourth lines rhyme. A limerick also has a special rhythm. Here is an example of a limerick:

> There once was a boy named Nash
> Who finished his math in a flash.
> He went out to play
> Outside for the day,
> And he ran a hundred-yard dash.

- A *concrete poem* takes the shape of its subject. Concrete poems may or may not rhyme. Here is an example of a concrete poem:

```
A R E C T A N G L E H A S F O
S                           U
E                           R
L                           S
G                           I
N                           D
A T H G I R R U O F D N A S E
```

DATA SHEET 15.3

Tips for Poets

Writers use many techniques when writing poems. Following are some of the most common.

Alliteration is the use of words with the same beginning sounds. Examples:

- Fred feels fractions are fun.
- Hailey hopes to get a hundred on her math test.

Figures of speech include similes, metaphors, and personification.

- *Similes* use the word *like* or *as* to compare things. Examples:

  Math is like an adventure.
  Alicia multiplies as fast as a calculator.

- *Metaphors* do not use the word *like* or *as* to compare things. Examples:

  Graphs are stories about numbers.
  The math test was a monster.

- In *personification*, human qualities are given to nonhuman things. Examples:

  Rebecca's math book called to her.
  My math homework waited for me.

Writing and Presenting Math Messages

WHEN YOU PROVIDE STUDENTS with the time and opportunity for communication about math, you elevate the awareness of math in your classroom, and the possibility for new insights and understanding increases. In this project, students share math messages—brief, informative packets of information that highlight math in some way. Both the message givers and their listeners benefit.

Goal

Working in groups of three or four, students are to write and present daily math messages of a few sentences to a paragraph or two. Each group will be responsible for a series of messages. The messages will be delivered at the beginning of math class. *Suggested time:* two to three class periods for researching and developing the math messages, and a few minutes each day for presentation of the messages.

Skills Covered

1. Specific math skills will vary depending on the content of students' math messages
2. Communicating mathematical ideas
3. Using technology (if computers are used)

Special Materials and Equipment

Reference books about math and 5-by-8-inch index cards. Optional: computers with Internet access.

Development

- This project can be developed and implemented in a variety of ways. First, you must decide how many math messages each group will be responsible for. You might have each group provide the math messages for one week of school, which means each group will be responsible for five messages; or you might prefer to have each group member be responsible for providing one message per day. Depending on the abilities of your students, you might ask the groups to provide more or fewer messages.

- Next, you must decide when and how often the groups will present their messages. Ideally, one message should be presented at the beginning of math class each day. As noted, the groups may take turns being responsible for presenting the messages for one week at a time. Another option is to have students sign up for specific days they would like to present a math message. This option works well if the groups choose topics that are tied to the calendar in some way—for example, sharing a math message about a famous mathematician on his or her birthday, or reporting on an event related to math that happened on a specific day.

- Before beginning the project, you also need to decide on the type of material you want your students to focus on in their math messages. Obviously the content of the messages can be broad, including just about anything related to math; or the content can be limited to specific topics, procedures, hints, tips, or items of math news. Perhaps you will have your students focus their messages on material they are currently studying or have studied. Knowing what material you want your students to cover in their math messages will help you point them in the right direction at the beginning of the project.

- Begin the project by explaining to your students that they are to work in groups and create math messages that they will present to the class. Make clear that each message is to be based on or related to math and is to be a few sentences to a paragraph or two.

- Hand out copies of Student Guide 16.1 and review with your students the information it presents. Explain how many messages each group is to provide. Inform them that the groups are to present messages on successive days, or instruct them to sign up on a calendar to present a math message on particular days. Keeping the calendar on display in the classroom allows students to check when they are to present a message, and makes it easy for you to remind them.

- Distribute copies of Data Sheet 16.2: Possible Topics for Math Messages. Review with your students the list of topics on the data sheet and instruct them to create their own list of topics for math messages. Emphasize that the topics on the data sheet are only a sample. There are many more topics they may discover on their own. Before they begin researching any topic, they should show their list of topics to you for your approval. Some topics may be too complex for a math message and others may be too simple. Also, make certain that different groups do not do the same topics.

- Hand out copies of Data Sheet 16.3: Examples of Math Messages. Go over the examples with your students. Point out that a math message should be brief and should highlight the most important information about the topic.

- Encourage your students to research their topics if necessary. Their math text book is a good source, but encourage them to consult other reference books as well. If possible, reserve time in the library for them to conduct research. Depending on their abilities and if they have Internet access, you may also encourage them to check online sources.

- Instruct your students to organize their information and write rough drafts of their messages. They should edit and revise their messages, and double-check any math facts. You should read the messages for clarity and accuracy before your students share them with the class. Suggest that they write the final copies of their messages on index cards. During their presentation they can refer to the cards.

- Explain that a math message will be presented at the beginning of math class each day. Make certain that students know when their group is to present their messages.

- To ensure that your students do not misplace their messages between when they complete them and when they are to present them, you may collect the index cards from each group for safekeeping, then return them when the group's members are to present their messages.

- During the presentations, the group member presenting the message should either stand before the class or sit at his or her desk.

Wrap Up

Encourage the rest of your students to comment or ask questions about the math message presented. At this point, other members of the group besides the presenter may answer questions or offer additional information.

Extensions

Make math messages an ongoing activity in your class. Once your students gain experience in researching, writing, and presenting math messages, the process will be easier.

You might also send the messages your students create to other teachers in your school via e-mail. They can then share your students' math messages with their own students. Be sure that credit is given to the creators of the math messages.

STUDENT GUIDE 16.1

Writing and Presenting Math Messages

Project

Your group is to create math messages. You will present your finished math messages to your classmates. Your messages may be a few sentences or a paragraph or two in length.

Key Steps

1. Brainstorm and make a list of possible topics for your math messages. Data Sheet 16.2 contains some ideas. You can also check your math textbook. If possible, check math Web sites for ideas.

2. Divide the tasks of this project among the group's members. Some students may research ideas. Others may write the messages. Someone else may check the math facts. Others may present the messages to the class.

3. Learn as much about your topics as possible through research. Your math text will be a good source. Reference books about math are also sources of information.

4. Double-check the math facts. They must be correct.

5. Write the final copy of your math messages on index cards. Use your index cards when you present your messages to the class.

Special Tips

- Make sure that each idea on your list is suitable for a math message. Some topics may be too big. Other topics may be too small. Choose the best ideas that interest you the most.

- Remember that you will share your math messages with the class. Your messages must be written clearly. Edit and revise your messages. Read them out loud to make sure they are clear.

- You may choose different people to present different messages.

- After your presentation, be ready to answer questions about your math messages.

To Be Submitted

Written copies of your math messages

DATA SHEET 16.2

Possible Topics for Math Messages

You may be able to create math messages for some of the following topics:

News about math

Special days or weeks (for example, National Metric Week)

Math on this day in history

Study tips (for math tests and quizzes)

Ways to check your computation

Common mistakes in math and how to avoid them

Problem-solving strategies

Tips for solving word problems

Types of numbers

Types of fractions

Tips for working with fractions

Operations (for example, order of operations)

Measurement (customary and metric)

Time and time zones

Types of graphs

Geometric figures

Famous mathematicians (their birthdays and achievements)

Math puzzlers (for example, why a square is a rectangle but a rectangle is not a square)

DATA SHEET 16.3

Examples of Math Messages

A math message must be brief and clear. It should share important facts about math. Following are two examples.

How to Solve a Word Problem

Read the problem and be sure you understand it. Read it again if you have to. Decide what you must solve for. Find the numbers you need to solve the problem. Make a plan to solve the problem. Follow your plan and solve the problem. Check your answer to see if it makes sense.

Gabriel Daniel Fahrenheit

Gabriel Daniel Fahrenheit was born on May 14, 1686. He invented the Fahrenheit temperature scale. On the Fahrenheit scale, water freezes at 32 degrees and boils at 212 degrees. The normal temperature of the human body is 98.6 degrees. The Fahrenheit temperature scale is still used today.

Writing and Performing Math Skits

STUDENTS WHO ASSUME an active role in their learning often learn more easily than students who take a passive role. In this project, students literally take an active role as they act out math skits.

Goal

Working in groups of three or four, students are to write and perform a short skit about math. *Suggested time:* two to three class periods to create skits and another period to perform them.

Skills Covered

1. Various math skills depending on the content of students' skits
2. Communicating ideas about math
3. Using technology (if computers are used)

Special Materials and Equipment

Props that students may create or obtain to support their performance in their skits. Optional: computers and printers.

Development

• Before introducing this project to your students, consider guidelines. For example, we suggest that you limit the skits to between two and four minutes. This is long enough for students to do a short skit on a topic in math, but not so long that they will feel pressured to fill the time requirements with empty dialogue. Of course, depending on the abilities of your students, you can adjust these times. Also, consider the types of props you will allow. Some students can become quite excited with this kind of project and quickly go overboard if not given clear boundaries. We suggest that any props be simple—objects that can be easily obtained or made. Many of the props they will need will probably already be in your classroom.

• Start this project by explaining to your students that they will work in groups of three or four and write and present skits about math. Explain that a skit is a short presentation that is acted out. It is similar to a play but shorter. Mention that the skits will be performed in the classroom.

• Hand out copies of Student Guide 17.1 and review the information it presents with your students. Make clear that their skits are to be between two and four minutes, and that all members of the group should participate as actors or as narrators. Also note that any props they want to use should be readily available or easy to make. Emphasize that the skits are to be about math. Suggest that students focus on helpful hints, study tips, insights, or practical advice; however, possible topics are just about limitless. You might also want to caution your students that the skits should be positive. Otherwise you might see a skit in which students lament the amount of math homework they receive.

• Hand out copies of Data Sheet 17.2: Sample Skit. Read the skit with your students. Call their attention to the structure of the skit, which is similar to the structure of a play but simplified. Point out that the characters are listed at the top, the setting is described, the dialogue of the characters is clearly shown, and stage directions are placed in parentheses. Explain that when written in this manner, the characters' lines are easy to read and learn.

• Distribute copies of Worksheet 17.3: Skit Ideas. Explain that every skit follows a plan, similar to the plan for plays. The skit opens with the characters facing a problem. Then the characters try to solve the problem. (In the typical play, the characters face complications that make solving the problem harder and can lead to more problems.) The characters eventually solve (or fail to solve) the problem. Answering the questions on the worksheet will help your students to identify the essential ingredients of their skits.

• Instruct your students to follow the structure of the sample skit on Data Sheet 17.2 when writing their skits. Note that they should provide a title, list their characters, and describe a setting. The names of the characters should be written in capital letters and followed by colons. Any stage directions should be placed in parentheses, and the dialogue should be written in the way the characters would really speak.

• Encourage your students to make or obtain props for their skits. We recommend that you instruct them to check with you before working on any props. Steer them away from trying to obtain or make props that might be expensive, overly complex, or difficult to handle.

• Encourage your students to begin by writing rough drafts of their skits, then edit and revise them. Also remind them that any math facts they use in their skits must be correct.

• Depending on your students' abilities and their access to computers, encourage them to write their skits on a computer. They can then print out enough copies for all group members.

• If your students write their skits in longhand, make enough photocopies for each member of the group.

• Encourage your students to practice their skits. Provide some class time for each group to rehearse. Although all members of the group should have a part, you may find that some students are shy or reluctant to perform in front of their classmates. Rather than force such students to participate, perhaps you can have them narrate.

• When it comes time to present the skits, you may allow students to read their lines from a copy of the skit. This relieves anxiety about having to memorize.

Wrap Up

Have students perform their skits.

Extension

Videotape the skits. Play the tape in class so your students can see their performances. Note: before videotaping students, be sure to check your school's policies regarding videotaping and obtain your administrator's approval. You may also need to obtain written permission from parents to videotape their children.

STUDENT GUIDE 17.1

Writing and Performing Math Skits

Project

Your group is to write a skit about math. You will then act out the skit for your class.

Key Steps

1. Brainstorm and make a list of possible ideas for your math skit. Your skit might offer advice for math homework. It might be about a shortcut in math. Maybe it will show the importance of math.

2. Choose the idea you like best and discuss the best ways to develop your skit. Use Worksheet 17.3 to develop your ideas.

3. Decide who your characters will be. Also decide what problem they must solve, and how they will solve the problem.

4. Decide who your narrator will be. The narrator will introduce the skit, read the list of characters, and describe the setting.

5. Write your skit following the structure provided on Data Sheet 17.2. First write a draft, then edit and revise your skit.

6. Make or obtain props for your skit.

7. Rehearse your skit. Make sure that everyone knows his or her part.

Special Tips

- All props should be simple and easy to handle.

To Be Submitted

A copy of your skit

DATA SHEET 17.2

Sample Skit

Following is a sample skit entitled *Double-Check*.

Characters

> Jillian, nine years old
> Paulo, ten years old
> Maria, nine years old

Setting

School lunch room. The characters are sitting at a table eating lunch. Jillian looks worried.

MARIA (looks at Jillian): Is something wrong?

JILLIAN (frowning): I don't know if I did our math homework right.

PAULO: You mean the long division?

JILLIAN: We were supposed to check our answers, but I'm not sure how.

PAULO: It's easy. (He takes a pen from his pocket and writes a problem on his brown paper lunch bag.) You multiply the quotient by the divisor and add the remainder. That gives you the dividend.

JILLIAN (puzzled): The what? By the what? Gives you the what?

MARIA: I see. It's the terms that confuse you. The quotient is the answer. The divisor is the number you divide by. And the dividend is the number you divide into.

PAULO: Right. And the remainder is the number left over after you divide.

JILLIAN (smiling): Oh, now I get it. It's easy.

THE END

Skit Ideas

Answer the following questions. The answers will help you to write your skit.

1. What is the topic of your skit?

_____

_____

2. Who are the lead characters?

_____

_____

_____

_____

3. Describe the problem the characters face.

_____

_____

_____

_____

4. Describe how the characters solve the problem.

_____

_____

_____

_____

5. Describe any props you will need for your skit.

_____

_____

_____

Writing Math Word Problems for Other Students

TEACHERS ALWAYS PROVIDE WORK for their students. In this project, your students get a chance to provide work for one another in the form of word problems. Writing math word problems also helps students get better at solving word problems.

Goal

Working in pairs or groups of three, students will write at least five math word problems that will be given to other students to solve. *Suggested time:* two to three class periods.

Skills Covered

1. Various math skills depending on the content of the word problems
2. Understanding how to solve word problems
3. Using technology in problem solving (if computers or calculators are used)

Special Materials and Equipment

White $8\frac{1}{2}$-by-11-inch paper. Optional: computers, printers, and calculators.

Development

- Before introducing this project to your students, consider how you wish to develop it. For example, you may prefer to have your students write word problems that focus on the current unit of study, or you may give them more latitude by encouraging them to write problems on any topic the class has already studied. Consider whether you will allow groups to exchange copies of their problems with each other or instead collect what you feel are the best problems and distribute them to the class. Answering such questions in advance will enable you to provide your students with clear directions as the project progresses.

- Start this project by explaining to your students that they will work in pairs or groups of three to write word problems for their classmates. Note that at the end of the project students will exchange their problems with one another and solve the problems written by their classmates.

- Distribute copies of Student Guide 18.1 and review the information it presents with your students. Note that they are to write at least five word problems, although you may encourage them to write more. Also note any specific topics they are to consider or if they may choose their own topics.

- Distribute copies of Data Sheet 18.2: Guidelines for Writing Math Word Problems. Review the suggestions with your students and note that the problems they write should be geared to the general level of the class. Otherwise some students might create problems that are much too simple or much too difficult.

- Explain that students should first write rough copies of their problems, then edit and revise the problems and double-check all the math. In addition, they must provide an answer key. You may suggest that they use calculators when checking their math and creating the key.

- Explain to your students that they should write the final copies of their problems on white paper using dark pencil or ink, which will result in clear photocopies.

- Depending on the abilities of your students and their access to computers, you may encourage them to write their problems on a computer. Many software programs provide math symbols and the means for writing fractions and equations and drawing geometric figures. Although such programs can be somewhat demanding for young students, for other students they can be a wonderful option.

- Be sure to proofread all final copies of problems before photocopying them. Either make copies of each group's problems for distribution to the class or choose the best one or two problems from each group and create a sheet of these. Make enough copies for all of the students in your class.

- You may wish to hand out copies of Data Sheet 18.3: Guidelines for Solving Math Word Problems, which can be helpful to your students as they solve the problems written by their classmates.

Wrap Up

Have your students solve the word problems written by their classmates.

Extension

Instruct your students to create review word problems for upcoming quizzes or tests.

STUDENT GUIDE 18.1

Writing Math Word Problems for Other Students

Project

You and your partner or group are to create a worksheet of word problems. You must write at least five word problems for your classmates to solve.

Key Steps

1. Each member of the group should write two or three ideas for word problems.

2. Discuss the ideas, then choose the best ones.

3. Use the tips on Data Sheet 18.2 to help you write your problems.

4. Write a rough copy of your word problems. Edit and revise your writing and double-check your math to make sure that all facts are correct.

5. On your final copy, leave space between the problems for students to do the math. Write your problems in black ink or dark pencil. Add figures or diagrams if they are necessary.

6. Remember to write an answer key for your problems.

Special Tips

- Think about word problems you have solved. Check your textbook for examples. Use these problems as guides for writing your own.

- Decide how to organize your worksheet. For example, which problem should be first? Which problems should be second, third, and fourth? Which problem should be last?

- Do not create problems that are too hard or too easy for your classmates.

- Make sure that your writing is clear.

- Any figures or diagrams should be drawn neatly and labeled clearly.

- If possible, write your problems on a computer. This will make revision easier.

To Be Submitted

A copy of your worksheet and your answer key

DATA SHEET 18.2

Guidelines for Writing Math Word Problems

Solving word problems can be challenging. Writing word problems can be even more challenging. Following are some tips.

1. Problems should be based on real-life situations.

2. Problems should have all the information needed to solve them.

3. Problems should ask clear questions.

4. Problems should be written clearly.

5. Problems should focus on math skills that students already have. Otherwise they will not be able to solve the problems.

6. Different problems should use different operations. Problem 1 may use addition. Problem 2 may use multiplication. Problem 3 may use subtraction. Problem 4 may use division.

7. Problems may have one, two, or three steps. Remember that the more steps a problem has, the harder it is to solve.

8. Some problems should be easy. Some should be hard. Maybe make the last problem a challenge.

9. Problems should be written with correct grammar and punctuation.

10. All spelling should be correct.

DATA SHEET 18.3

Guidelines for Solving Math Word Problems

Here are some tips that will help you to solve word problems.

1. Read the problem carefully. You may need to read it two, three, or more times. Make sure you understand the problem.

2. Decide what the problem is asking you to find.

3. Find the facts you will need to solve the problem.

4. Decide on a plan to solve the problem. You might use one of the following methods:

   - Draw a picture.
   - Find a pattern.
   - Make a graph.
   - Make a list.
   - Make a model.
   - Make a table.
   - Do guess and check.
   - Solve a simpler problem.
   - Work backward.

5. Decide what operation you will use: addition? subtraction? multiplication? division? Will you need to use more than one operation?

6. Work out the problem.

7. Double-check your work.

8. Ask yourself if your answer makes sense. If it does not, recheck your work.

Math Journals

MATH JOURNALS PROVIDE a fine opportunity for students to write about their experiences with math. Journals can become a storehouse and showcase of students' opinions, impressions, and feelings about math; their ponderings; their solutions to specific problems; and their observations about concepts or skills, insights, and ah-ha moments. Journals can be where students think about math and write down their thoughts.

Math journals often show a side of students that teachers otherwise rarely see. They can be an important, ongoing activity in your class.

Goal

Each student will maintain a math journal for an extended time, perhaps a marking period, a semester, or the entire school year. *Suggested time:* one class period (or partial period) to introduce the project; students will then write in their journals on their own.

Skills Covered

1. Various math skills depending on the content of students' journal entries
2. Writing as a means to express ideas about math
3. Making connections between math and other subjects

Special Materials and Equipment

A composition or similar notebook for each student to use as a journal.

Development

- Before introducing this project to your students, prepare some basic guidelines. Although some students will write in their math journals regularly without prompting, others may write in their journals reluctantly. To address this problem, some teachers require their students to write in their journals a specific number of times. For example, students may be required to write in their math journals about assigned topics at least twice each week, which is enough to provide them with a sense of continuity without overwhelming them. Of course some students will write in their journals more frequently.

- Decide in advance what topics, if any, you want your students to focus on. Many teachers prefer to leave topic choice entirely up to their students, as long as it is related to math.

- Decide how often you will review your students' journals. It is unrealistic to try to read every journal each day. Instead, plan on reading some journals a few times each week, making sure that you periodically read all of them. When you read the journals, focus on your students' ideas and not on mechanics, that is, on grammar, punctuation, and spelling. If you concentrate on mechanics, your students will too and their attention on math will lessen. Respond to the ideas of your students. Offer encouragement and suggestions, and ask questions to help them think more deeply about their topics. Math journals are places where ideas about math are shared.

- Start this project by explaining to your students that each of them is to maintain a math journal. If they have no experience with math journals, explain to them that a math journal is a book in which they can write about math. Offer some examples, such as they may write about their attempts at solving specific problems, concerns they have about learning math, opinions, shortcuts they have discovered—just about anything in math that is of importance to them. Make clear how often you expect them to write in their journals, but encourage them to write more often if they wish.

- Distribute copies of Student Guide 19.1 and review the information provided with your students. Mention if there are any specific topics you wish them to address, and note that you will collect their journals periodically. Explain that math journals should not be used for any other subject. Also explain that although you will respect their private thoughts about math, you must report anything you read that you feel might endanger the student or someone else.

- Hand out copies of Data Sheet 19.2: Guidelines for Keeping Math Journals, which offers tips on how to maintain a math journal as well as topics students may wish to write about. Keep in mind that some students may need more direction than others. You may also find it helpful to discuss additional ideas for journal entries.

Wrap Up

Read your students' journals regularly and respond to their writing. If you notice similar themes or concerns among the journals, address them in class while respecting the privacy of students and not mentioning names.

Extension

Make this project ongoing throughout the school year. At the end of the year, suggest that your students reread their entries. It is likely that they will be surprised at their progress in learning math.

STUDENT GUIDE 19.1

Math Journals

Project

You will write about math topics in a journal.

Key Steps

1. Think about ideas you would like to write about in your journal. See Data Sheet 19.2 for general ideas.

2. Write in your journal as often as you can. Write in your journal at home as well as at school.

3. Be sure to write about topics your teacher assigns.

4. Remember that your teacher will collect and read your journal. Keep your journal up-to-date.

5. Reread your journal entries from time to time. This will help you see your progress in learning math.

Special Tips

- Remember that all entries in your math journal must be about math.
- Bring your math journal to class each day.

To Be Submitted

Your math journal

DATA SHEET 19.2

Guidelines for Keeping Math Journals

1. Write your name on your journal. If you run out of space, start another journal. Number your journals.

2. Always date your entries.

3. Write about topics in math that interest you.

4. Explore your ideas, thoughts, and feelings about math in your journal.

5. Use your journal to show your growth in math.

Possible Ideas and Topics for Math Journals

- Things I like (or dislike) about math
- Steps for solving a tough problem
- A shortcut I learned
- A concept I finally understand
- A new skill
- A time I helped another student learn math
- Feelings before a big test
- Study tips
- A time I needed to know math
- Feelings about a topic or problem
- A skill I found easy
- A way I remember a math rule
- My favorite topic in math
- Current topics in my math class: homework problems, classwork, studying for a test or quiz

Chapter Seven

Math and Art

Creating a Billboard That Advertises Math

BILLBOARDS FREQUENTLY DOT the landscape along major highways. They are a method of advertising that presents brief messages to the public. In this project, students can create a billboard of their own that shares a message about math.

Goal

Working in pairs or groups of three, students will create a math billboard. *Suggested time:* two to three class periods.

Skills Covered

1. Various math skills depending on the content of students' billboards
2. Communicating ideas about math
3. Using art to convey ideas about math
4. Measuring lengths
5. Using technology (if computers are used)

Special Materials and Equipment

Poster paper, rulers, compasses, scissors, glue, colored pencils, crayons, markers. Optional: computers with printers.

Development

• Discuss billboards with your students, explaining that they are roadside displays used for advertising. Ask them about some billboards they may recall seeing. Explain that most billboards are placed along highways or other well-traveled roads. Because people are driving, the message on a billboard must be brief. It must also be attractive and interesting enough to catch attention.

• Start this project by explaining that your students will work with a partner or in groups of three. They are to create a billboard on poster paper that shares an idea or message about math.

• Hand out copies of Student Guide 20.1 and review the information it provides with your students. Discuss the billboard ideas it suggests. If necessary, ask for volunteers to suggest other potential topics. Write their examples on the board or on an overhead screen. Seeing many possible ideas will help your students get started.

• Distribute copies of Data Sheet 20.2: Billboard Basics and go over the guidelines with your students. Suggest that they first do a rough sketch of their billboard on a sheet of paper. They should experiment with different designs by placing headlines, text, and pictures in various locations on the sheet.

• Hand out copies of Worksheet 20.3: Math Billboard Idea Sheet. Instruct your students to answer the questions on the worksheet, then use the information they provided in their answers in the design of the billboard.

• Caution your students not to include too much information on their billboards. Any written material should be brief as well as clear and to the point. People pass by billboards fast and do not have time to read information set in paragraphs. Likewise, complex pictures with too much detail should be avoided. An effective billboard is designed to catch the eye and deliver its message quickly.

• Emphasize the importance of neatness in making the billboards. If a billboard is sloppy or cluttered, its message may be lost. Suggest that your students use rulers for making straight lines, and compasses for making circles and arcs. Rulers should also be used to measure the positions of headlines, text, and pictures. If necessary, demonstrate the use of rulers and compasses to your students.

• Depending on your students' abilities and whether they have access to computers, encourage them to write their headlines and text on the computer. The various fonts, print sizes, and colors available can help them make their billboards stand out. Note that they can also cut out text and headlines they create and glue them onto their posters.

Wrap Up

Have the members of each group show their billboard to the class and comment on its message. Display your students' billboards in your classroom and in nearby hallways.

Extension

Display the billboards in a main lobby or central location when parents are visiting the school. Your students' billboards will make a great exhibit and share messages about math.

STUDENT GUIDE 20.1

Creating a Billboard That Advertises Math

Project

You and your partner or group are to create a billboard. Your billboard is to advertise math.

Key Steps

1. Think of math ideas to advertise. Check your math textbook and reference books for possible ideas. Here are some examples.

- Double-checking math answers
- Properties in math
- Estimating
- Simplifying fractions
- Geometric shapes

- Illustration of a formula
- Equivalent values
- Study tips
- Measurement
- Graphs

2. Discuss what you feel are the best ideas. Remember that you must be able to communicate your idea on a billboard. Some ideas may be too complicated.

3. Answer the questions on Worksheet 20.3 to help organize your thoughts for the billboard.

4. Divide the tasks for this project among your group's members. One person may be responsible for the written material. Another may be responsible for the art. A third may be responsible for double-checking all of the material.

5. Check your work on your billboard. Be sure all words are spelled correctly. Make sure all math is correct before you hand it in.

Special Tips

- Try different designs for your billboard. Sketch rough drafts on a sheet of paper. Decide which design is best for sharing your message.
- If possible, use a computer to write the text and headlines. Print out the material. Carefully cut it out and glue it onto the poster paper.

To Be Submitted

Your billboard

DATA SHEET 20.2

Billboard Basics

Billboards contain advertisements. The purpose of a billboard is to sell something or to share a message. Billboards are often placed along highways and busy roads. The following tips can help you design a billboard about math.

1. The message on a billboard must be brief and clear.

2. Most billboards have both words and pictures. Many have headlines.

3. The words and pictures must work together to create the message. The billboard should be balanced. Words and pictures should be spread across the billboard. They should not be set on only one side.

4. Lettering must be clear. All words must be spelled correctly.

5. Pictures should be drawn neatly. They should help communicate the message.

6. Colors can make billboards attractive. Choose colors for contrast. For example, blue and yellow will stand out against each other. Be careful about choosing similar colors. For example, blue and purple might blend together.

Math Billboard Idea Sheet

Answer the following questions. The answers will help you find ideas for your billboard.

1. What is the topic of your billboard?

   _____

   _____

   _____

   _____

2. What is the message you want to share on your billboard?

   _____

   _____

   _____

   _____

3. What, if any, headlines will you use?

   _____

   _____

   _____

   _____

4. Describe any pictures that will be on your billboard.

   _____

   _____

   _____

   _____

Additional notes:

_____

_____

Creating a Math Cartoon

MOST STUDENTS LIKE TO READ CARTOONS, and some also like to draw them. For this project they can tap into their creativity and create a cartoon of their own about math.

Goal

Working individually or in pairs, students are to create a cartoon that depicts math in a positive manner. *Suggested time:* two to three class periods.

Skills Covered

1. Various math skills depending on the ideas that students develop for their cartoons
2. Awareness of spatial relationships
3. Communicating ideas about math
4. Using technology (if computers are used)

Special Materials and Equipment

Drawing paper, black pens, rulers, crayons, colored pencils, markers, and samples of cartoons, particularly one-frame cartoons and comics. Optional: computers with Internet access.

Development

- For this project, you might consider working with your students' art teacher. You can focus on the mathematics of the cartoons; he or she can assist students with their drawings.

- Before you start the project, collect samples of one-frame (also called one-panel) cartoons and comics, such as *Family Circus, The Far Side,* or *Ziggy,* from newspapers. These are the kinds of cartoons your students should try to create. You may consider allowing them to draw cartoons of more than one frame; however, the storyline of multiframe cartoons can be difficult to manage, particularly for young students.

- Begin this project by explaining to your students that they will work individually or in pairs to create a one-frame cartoon that shares a message about math.

- Distribute the sample cartoons to your students. Many examples of math cartoons can also be found online. A search using the term *math cartoons* will result in numerous Web sites. Viewing examples of math cartoons can help your students think of ideas for their own cartoons. Discuss the various parts of the cartoons: the art, characters, dialogue, and background. Note any captions and speech balloons. Explain that cartoonists must be aware of spatial relationships, that is, the way the different parts of cartoons are arranged. Trying to fit too much on a cartoon can cause the message to be lost amid clutter. Note that most cartoons are designed to be amusing. They usually show a lighthearted situation and express their message in the form of the punch line of a joke.

- You can also access Web sites that offer general information about cartoons and how to create them. Using search terms such as *creating cartoons, cartoon making,* or *cartooning for kids* will lead to many useful Web sites. Caution: before you direct students to any cartoon Web sites, preview the sites to ensure that the content is appropriate for students of your grade level.

- Distribute copies of Student Guide 21.1 and review with your students the information provided. Note that their cartoons should express a message about math or show an amusing math-related situation. Instruct students to create a cartoon of one frame, or scene. If you prefer, you may allow advanced students to create multiframe cartoons.

- Hand out copies of Data Sheet 21.2: Cartoon Creations. Review the suggestions for designing and making cartoons and recommend that your students follow the suggestions when creating their own cartoons.

- Because you may have students who worry that they cannot draw well, explain that the cartoons will not be judged on the basis of the students' artistic ability, but rather on their overall design and message about math.

- Encourage your students to experiment with ideas for their cartoons. Suggest that they sketch rough copies before attempting to do a final copy. Explain that all elements of the cartoon should work together to express their ideas.

Hands-On Math Projects

Wrap Up

Display your students' cartoons in class.

Extensions

Suggest that your students create more complex cartoons, perhaps comic strips of four frames. You may also publish a class math cartoon book.

STUDENT GUIDE 21.1

Creating a Math Cartoon

Project

You or you and your partner are to create a cartoon. Your cartoon will share a message or amusing scene about math.

© Randy Glasbergen. www.glasbergen.com

"How can I trust your information when you're using such outdated technology?"

Key Steps

1. Study examples of cartoons. Discuss their settings, characters, and dialogue.
2. List possible ideas for your cartoon. Choose the one you think is best.
3. See Data Sheet 21.2 for tips on creating your cartoon.
4. Draw the final copy of your cartoon as neatly as you can. Use a ruler to make straight lines.

Special Tips

- Make sure your idea can be expressed in one frame.
- Make rough sketches of your ideas. Balance the background and characters. You may need to try different designs. Remember to leave room for captions and dialogue.
- Use quotation marks or speech balloons to show dialogue. Choose the words of your characters carefully.

To Be Submitted

Your cartoon

DATA SHEET 21.2

Cartoon Creations

A cartoon is an amusing drawing. Most cartoons have a message. There are many kinds of cartoons. The following tips can help you to create a cartoon about math.

1. Think of an idea for your cartoon. You should be able to share the idea in both art and words.

2. Think of a scene that can help you express your idea. This will be your setting.

3. Think of characters for your cartoon. Characters can be people, animals, or objects.

4. Your cartoon may have captions and dialogue.

   • Captions help tell your story. They are usually placed at the bottom of a cartoon. They describe the action or scene.
   • Dialogue is the words spoken by the characters. Sometimes dialogue is shown in speech balloons. Sometimes it is shown in quotation marks.

5. Think of a punch line. A punch line may be an amusing message or the end of a joke.

6. Carefully design your cartoon. Leave enough space for speech balloons and captions.

7. Draw your cartoon neatly.

8. Add color to make your cartoon more interesting.

9. Make sure your message is clear.

Painting a T-Shirt with a Math Slogan

I N AN EFFORT to promote mathematics, the National Council of Teachers of Mathematics designates April as Mathematics Awareness Month. Of course math teachers promote math in their classrooms every day. To celebrate Mathematics Awareness Month, or to celebrate a special math event in your school, your students can create a math slogan and paint it on a T-shirt.

Goal

Working in groups of three or four, students will create a math slogan in observation of a special math event. They will then paint the slogan on a T-shirt. *Suggested time:* three to four class periods.

Skills Covered

1. Various math skills depending on the T-shirt slogans
2. Synthesizing information related to math
3. Communicating ideas about math

Special Materials and Equipment

One washed white T-shirt per student (which you may provide or require your students to bring in); one 1-foot-by-2-foot piece of cardboard per student to prevent the colors of the slogan from seeping through to the other side of the T-shirt;

rulers, masking tape, scissors, heavy drawing paper, fabric markers or fabric paints, and brushes; plastic (or garbage bags) to cover desks or tables; disposable wipes for cleaning hands. Optional: an iron to set the paint, depending on the paint manufacturer's instructions.

Development

- Before you begin this project, visit a local craft store and decide whether you will purchase fabric markers or fabric paints for your students' T-shirts. Consider the price, and whether markers or paints will be easier for your students to use. Also consider any manufacturer's guidelines. Some, for example, recommend that their paints and markers be used in a well-ventilated area. Other manufacturers require that the painted T-shirts be ironed in order for the paints to set. Also note that some paints are not odor free and may trigger allergies, asthma, or headaches in some students. Check with your school nurse to find out if she has any information regarding students who might be adversely affected by the materials you will be using. Finally, estimate the total costs for materials and, if necessary, get approval from supervisors and obtain funds from your school to cover the costs.

- Consider collaborating with your students' art teacher for this project. He or she may have some of the supplies you will need or may do similar types of activities as part of the art curriculum. The art teacher can be a great resource, helping with the painting and maybe even allowing students to paint their T-shirts in the art room.

- Begin this project by discussing slogans with your students. Point out that slogans are often found on shirts as a form of advertising. Ask your students if they know of any slogans. It is likely they can share several.

- Explain that students are to work in groups to design a math slogan, and that each student will paint their group's slogan on a T-shirt and wear it on the day of a special math event.

- Hand out copies of Student Guide 22.1 and review the information it contains with your students. Emphasize that their slogans should be simple but should highlight math in some way. Discuss the samples provided. Depending on your students' abilities, you might have them volunteer more ideas.

- Distribute copies of Data Sheet 22.2: How to Paint a T-Shirt and go over the information it provides. If your students are responsible for bringing in their own T-shirts, emphasize that the shirts must be white and washed. (Even brand new T-shirts must be washed because the paint or markers will adhere better to washed fabric.) Remind your students to write their name on a strip of masking tape and attach the tape to the inside of the T-shirt, in the back, near the neck. Instruct them to follow the guidelines on the data sheet closely as they paint their T-shirts. (Note: depending on your students' abilities, you may prefer to cut the cardboard for them in advance.)

- Instruct your students to sketch the letters of their slogans on drawing paper. Encourage them to experiment with different types of lettering and different designs until they find a design they like. Explain that their letters should be big enough to communicate their slogan, but not so big that they spread too far across the T-shirt, making the slogan hard to read. Note that they should choose colors for their letters that enhance their slogan.

• After they have decided on a final form for the letters of their slogan, instruct your students to make a final copy of the letters on heavy drawing paper. (They should retain their original sketches for reference.)

• Remind your students to show you their final copies before they cut out the letters, so you can make sure their slogans are ready to be placed on their T-shirts.

• After you hand back their final copies, instruct your students to cut out the letters. These letters will serve as patterns for drawing the letters on their T-shirts. Suggest that they use a ruler to measure the space between the letters when placing the letters on their T-shirts.

• As your students paint their T-shirts, circulate around the room and provide help as necessary. Caution them to be careful when painting so they do not stain their clothing or themselves. Make sure they place the cardboard inside their shirts; otherwise the colors on one side may bleed through to the other side. Some students will also need help placing and painting the letters of the slogans on their T-shirts.

• When your students are finished painting their T-shirts, allow the shirts time and space to dry thoroughly according to the paint manufacturer's directions. Avoid placing the shirts on top of each other because this may cause the paint to smear.

Wrap Up

Have your students wear their T-shirts to celebrate an event in math.

Extension

Your students may wish to incorporate an illustration into the design of their T-shirts in addition to their slogans.

STUDENT GUIDE 22.1

Painting a T-Shirt with a Math Slogan

Project

Your group will create a math slogan. Each member will paint the group's slogan on his or her white T-shirt.

Key Steps

1. Think about slogans you have heard or seen. Discuss them with your group's members. Discuss why people remember some slogans better than others.

2. Brainstorm ideas for your math slogan. Here are some examples:

   - The Numbers Game

   - Got a Problem? Just Solve It

   - Prime Your Math Skills

   - Math Is Fun

   - Math Is 4 Me

3. Discuss the slogans you have come up with. Pick your favorite to put on your T-shirt.

4. Sketch rough copies of your slogan. Use different forms of lettering. Try different designs. Revise your designs until you are satisfied. Double-check your spelling.

5. Make a final copy of your slogan on drawing paper. Hand it in to your teacher for his or her approval.

6. After your teacher returns your final copy, carefully cut out the letters of your slogan. You and the members of your group will use these letters as patterns for painting on your T-shirt.

7. Follow the instructions on Data Sheet 22.2 to paint your slogan on your T-shirt.

Special Tips

- Try to pick a slogan that people will remember easily.

- Choose a slogan that is simple. Fewer words are better.

- Pick colors to highlight your slogan.

To Be Submitted

The final copy of your slogan

DATA SHEET 22.2

How to Paint a T-Shirt

The following tips can help you paint your slogan on a T-shirt:

1. Bring in a washed white T-shirt. Write your name on a piece of masking tape. Place the masking tape on the inside back of the T-shirt, near the neck.

2. Cover your desk or table with plastic. This will protect the surface from the paints.

3. Decide if you want the slogan to be on the front or back of your shirt.

4. Put a 1-foot-by-2-foot piece of cardboard inside your T-shirt. This will stop the colors from soaking through to the other side of the shirt.

5. Place the letters that form your slogan onto your T-shirt. The letters will be your pattern. Use a ruler to measure the distance between the letters. You can also use a ruler for drawing straight lines.

6. Use a pencil to lightly trace around the letters.

7. Hold your T-shirt up. Check to make sure your slogan is written clearly. Make sure all of your letters are evenly spaced. Make any final changes before coloring or painting.

8. Neatly color or paint the letters.

9. Let your T-shirt dry.

10. Wear your T-shirt and share your slogan about math.

Exploring Tangrams

ATANGRAM IS A CHINESE PUZZLE consisting of seven geometric pieces called *tans*. The tans can be fit together to form various shapes. Along with being challenging and amusing, tangrams can foster understanding of geometric figures, enhance spatial perception, and sharpen ability in visualization. Tangrams have been entertaining people for hundreds of years, and can be the take-off point for a fine math project.

Goal

Working in pairs or groups of three, students will create a tangram. They will explore the tans and arrange them into several forms. They will sketch the forms and name them. *Suggested time:* two class periods.

Skills Covered

1. Identifying specific geometric figures, including *triangles* (*right isosceles*), *squares*, *rectangles*, and *parallelograms*

2. Identifying specific geometric terms, including *line segment, point, vertex, midpoint, similar*, and *congruent*

3. Measuring with a ruler

4. Decomposing, rearranging, and visualizing shapes

5. Using technology (if computers are used)

Special Materials and Equipment

Heavy construction paper, rulers, and scissors. Optional: computers with Internet access.

Development

- Ask your students if they have ever played a math game or tried to solve a math puzzle. It is likely that most of them have. Explain that math-related puzzles have entertained, and frustrated, people for hundreds if not thousands of years. One of these puzzles is the tangram. You might like to share with your students *Grandfather Tang's Story: A Tale Told with Tangrams* by Ann Tompert (Perfection Learning, 1998). This short book can be an excellent introduction to tangrams.

- Start the project by explaining that a tangram is a Chinese puzzle made of seven geometric shapes: five triangles, a square, and a parallelogram. If necessary, review these figures with your students. Note that each piece of the puzzle is called a tan.

- Explain that students will work in pairs or groups of three. Together they will draw a tangram according to specific instructions, cut out the tans, and arrange the tans into various shapes.

- Hand out copies of Student Guide 23.1 and review the information with your students. Instruct them that they are to create at least three figures with their tans.

- Distribute copies of Data Sheet 23.2: Facts About Tangrams and go over the information with your students. Discuss the history of tangrams. Depending on your students' interests, you might mention that people such as Napoleon, Lewis Carroll, and Edgar Allan Poe enjoyed tangrams, which remain popular today. Make certain your students understand the geometric vocabulary of tangrams. Imagination and visualization play major roles in this project. Point out the sample shapes on the data sheet and make sure your students can identify them: a right triangle and a tree.

- Distribute copies of Data Sheet 23.3: How to Make a Tangram. Review the instructions with your students. Make sure they understand the terms *line, segment, midpoint,* and *vertex* and *vertices.* Emphasize the need for accurate measuring and careful cutting of the tans. If necessary, do the first few steps together as a class.

- Explain to your students that once they have created their tangrams and cut out the tans, they should explore and try to arrange the tans into at least three recognizable shapes, or more if they have time. Encourage them to use their imaginations when trying to arrange the tans into shapes. You might mention that there are thousands of possibilities. After they have arranged the tans into a recognizable shape, they should neatly sketch the shape on a separate sheet of paper. Their sketches should show the lines of the tans. Instruct your students to label each sketch.

Wrap Up

Encourage your students to share their sketches with others. You might also ask them to share any strategies they used in arranging the shapes, as well as their overall impressions of tangrams. Display the sketches.

Extension

Suggest that your students visit some of the many Web sites devoted to tangrams. A simple search using the term *tangram* will identify numerous sites. Many of the sites offer information on the history of tangrams, explorations, and games. (If students visit the Internet in class, be sure to circulate around the room to make sure they have found useful sites.)

STUDENT GUIDE 23.1

Exploring Tangrams

Project

You and your partner or group will draw a tangram. You will cut out the tans. You will use the tans to form at least three shapes.

Key Steps

1. Read the instructions for drawing your tangram on Data Sheet 23.3. Make sure you understand what you are to do.

2. Follow the instructions carefully.

3. Draw your tangram accurately. Carefully cut out each tan.

4. Try putting the tans back together into the shape of a square. This will help you see how the tans can be fit together.

5. Next try putting the tans together in different ways. Turning a figure can sometimes help you see a shape. Use your imagination. Try to see geometric figures, animals, plants, buildings, bridges, and common objects.

6. Sketch the shapes you see in your tans. Be sure to show the lines of each tan. Label each shape.

Special Tip

- Brainstorm. Discuss with your partner or group members what a particular figure might look like. Sometimes the ideas of other people can give you new ideas.

To Be Submitted

Sketches of at least three shapes you made with your tans

DATA SHEET 23.2
Facts About Tangrams

A tangram is a Chinese puzzle. It is made up of seven shapes: five triangles, a square, and a parallelogram. Each piece is called a tan. When the tans are put together in a special manner, they form a big square. The tans can also be put together in other ways to form many different shapes.

No one knows where or when the tangram was invented. Many people believe it was invented in China hundreds of years ago. According to one story, a servant of the Chinese emperor dropped an expensive square tile. The servant tried to put the pieces back together. He was unable to make a square, but he made several other shapes. This gave someone the idea for tangrams. In time the puzzle spread from China to other parts of the world. Tangrams reached America in the early 1800s.

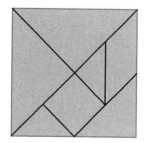

Following are more facts about tangrams:

- All of the triangles are similar.
- The two biggest triangles are congruent.
- The two smallest triangles are congruent.
- All of the triangles are right isosceles.

The seven tans can be put together to form thousands of shapes or pictures. Here are two examples:

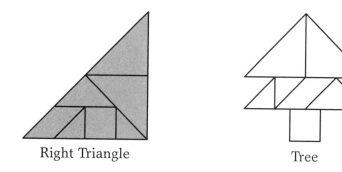

Right Triangle   Tree

173

DATA SHEET 23.3

How to Make a Tangram

1. Use a ruler to draw a square with sides of 4 inches.

2. Start at the upper left corner and label the vertices (corners) *A, B, C,* and *D* by moving right, down, and left. See the sample below.

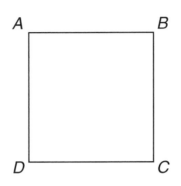

3. Draw line segment *BD*. Find the midpoint of line segment *BD* by measuring with your ruler. Label the midpoint *E*.

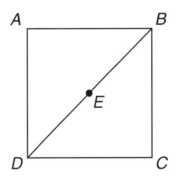

4. Draw line segment *AE*.

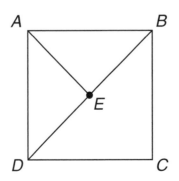

How to Make a Tangram *(Cont'd.)*

5. Find the midpoint of line segment *BC*. Label the midpoint *F*.
6. Find the midpoint of line segment *DC* and label the midpoint *G*.
7. Draw line segment *FG*.

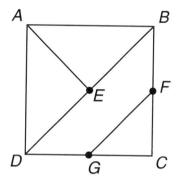

8. Find the midpoint of line segment *DE* and label it *H*.
9. Draw line segment *HG*.

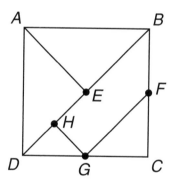

10. Find the midpoint of line segment *EB* and label it *I*.
11. Find the midpoint of line segment *FG* and label it *J*.
12. Draw line segments *IJ* and *EJ*.

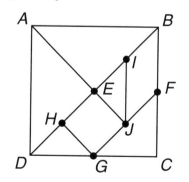

Cut neatly along the lines to make your tans. For a warm-up, try putting the tans back together to form the square again. Then try putting them together to form a rectangle. Use your imagination. Put your tans together to make more shapes or pictures.

Picture This
(Using Polygons to Model Fractions)

THE CONCEPT OF A FRACTION can be difficult for some students to understand. Models can help students visualize fractional parts and equivalent fractions. In this project, as students create models of fractions, they will gain insight into the relationships of parts to wholes.

Goal

Working in pairs or groups of three, students are to model fractions, equivalent fractions, or both using rectangles, squares, or other polygons. They are to create models out of construction paper, which can then be displayed in class. *Suggested time:* two to three class periods.

Skills Covered

1. Visualizing fractions as parts of a whole
2. Modeling fractions
3. Measuring lengths
4. Understanding types of polygons such as *squares, rectangles,* and *triangles*
5. Modeling equivalent fractions (optional)

Special Materials and Equipment

Large white construction paper on which models will be pasted; construction paper of various colors for the models; rulers, markers, glue, and scissors.

Development

• Review fractions with your students, emphasizing that fractions represent a part of a whole. Also review that equivalent fractions have the same value.

• Start this project by explaining to your students that they are to work with a partner or in a group of three to create models of fractions. You may also have them create models of equivalent fractions. Offer them the following example of a simple model of the fraction using a square.

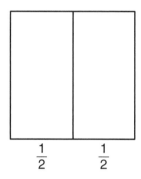

• Explain that in the example the square can be divided into two equal parts, as shown. Each of these parts equals $\frac{1}{2}$. Provide other examples if necessary.

• Hand out copies of Student Guide 24.1 and review the information it contains with your students. Note that they are to glue models of fractions onto white construction paper. They are to use different colors of construction paper to create the models to highlight the fractions. Encourage them to be artistic with their models.

• Distribute copies of Worksheet 24.2: Modeling Fractions and go over it with your students. You may have all of the groups create models of all of the examples of fractions and equivalent fractions on the worksheet, or you may assign only some fractions and equivalent fractions to each group. You may also add some fractions of your own to the assignment.

• Explain that the students may use squares, rectangles, or other polygons to model the fractions. Note that rectangles and squares will work well for most models. Although other polygons, such as triangles, parallelograms, rhombi, and so on, may make more interesting or attractive models, they may be more difficult to work with. If necessary, discuss them with your students.

• Explain that the students should first sketch their models on Worksheet 24.2, and then, after double-checking for accuracy, create their construction paper models. Models may vary; following are some examples:

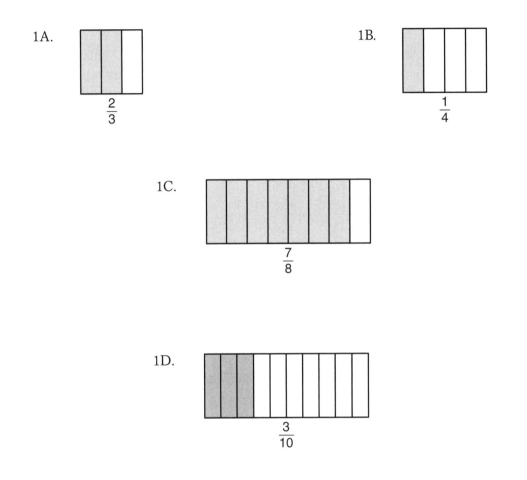

1A. $\frac{2}{3}$

1B. $\frac{1}{4}$

1C. $\frac{7}{8}$

1D. $\frac{3}{10}$

Following are models of equivalent fractions:

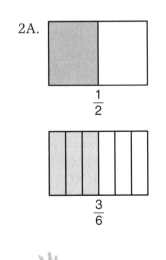

2A. $\frac{1}{2}$

$\frac{3}{6}$

2B.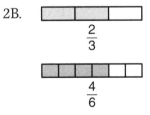

$\frac{2}{3}$

$\frac{4}{6}$

2C.

$\dfrac{4}{10}$

$\dfrac{2}{5}$

2D.

$\dfrac{6}{8}$

$\dfrac{3}{4}$

• Encourage your students to use rulers to ensure the accuracy of their models. If necessary, show them how to measure. Use a model of a square with sides of 4 inches, then divide it into halves. Note the importance of using units and measurements that can be easily divided. For example, a rectangle 4 inches long can easily be used to model $\dfrac{3}{4}$.

• Remind your students that they must label their models with the fractions the models represent.

Wrap Up

Display your students' models.

Extension

Instruct your students to model operations of fractions—addition, subtraction, multiplication, and division. For example, they might model $\dfrac{1}{5} + \dfrac{2}{5}$ or $\dfrac{1}{4} + \dfrac{1}{2}$.

Copyright © 2009 by Judith A. and Gary Robert Muschla

STUDENT GUIDE 24.1

Picture This (Using Polygons to Model Fractions)

Project

You and your partner or group are to create models that show fractions. You may use rectangles, squares, or other polygons in your models.

Key Steps

1. Decide which polygons to use to model fractions. Choose polygons that can easily be divided into equal parts. Squares or rectangles are good choices.

2. Sketch rough copies of your models on Worksheet 24.2. Divide the polygons into fractional parts. Use accurate measurements.

3. Use white construction paper for the background of your models.

4. Choose contrasting colors of construction paper for your models. Good contrasting colors might be yellow and red, or blue and orange. Similar colors, such as blue and purple, may not show the equal parts of fractions clearly.

5. Use rulers to draw the outlines of your square, rectangle, or other polygon. Then carefully measure and cut out the fractional parts of the figures you drew.

6. Glue the figures onto the white construction paper. Be sure your model shows the correct number of fractional parts.

7. Use markers to label your fractions.

Special Tip

• Arrange the models attractively on your background paper.

To Be Submitted

Your models of fractions

Name _____   Date _____

Modeling Fractions

1. Sketch a model of each of the following fractions.

   A. $\frac{2}{3}$

   B. $\frac{1}{4}$

   C. $\frac{7}{8}$

   D. $\frac{3}{10}$

2. Sketch a model to show that each of the following is true.

   A. $\frac{1}{2} = \frac{3}{6}$

   B. $\frac{2}{3} = \frac{4}{6}$

   C. $\frac{4}{10} = \frac{2}{5}$

   D. $\frac{6}{8} = \frac{3}{4}$

Making a Tessellation

M.C. ESCHER WAS A DUTCH ARTIST known for drawing *tessellations*, designs formed by a repeating pattern of closed figures that cover a surface. The figures that make a tessellation can be arranged in any manner, as long as they do not overlap and no spaces are left between them. In this project, your students will create a tessellation of their own.

Goal

Working individually, students will create a tessellation using some of the figures on Data Sheets 25.2, 25.3, and 25.4. In addition, they will write a brief description of their tessellation. *Suggested time:* two to three class periods.

Skills Covered

1. Identifying figures that will tessellate
2. Using patterns
3. Using technology (if computers are used)

Special Materials and Equipment

Large white construction paper, rulers, scissors, markers, crayons, colored pencils, and glue. Optional: computers with Internet access.

Development

- Before starting this project, obtain examples of tessellations to show to your students. You can find pictures of tessellations in books about M. C. Escher, such as *M.C. Escher: His Life and Work* by J. L. Locher (Abrams, 1992). You can also easily check Web sites by searching on *M. C. Escher; Escher, tessellations;* or simply *tessellations.*
- Begin this project by introducing Maurits Cornelis Escher (1898–1972) to your students. Escher was a Dutch artist famous for his tessellations. Offer examples and point out that a tessellation is a design formed by covering a surface (or plane) with a repeating pattern of closed figures. Emphasize that the figures must cover the surface completely. Space must not appear between any of the figures, nor should any of the figures overlap.
- Depending on the abilities of your students and their access to computers, you may encourage them to visit Web sites about Escher and tessellations. They will no doubt be fascinated by the art.
- Explain that for this project students are to work individually to create a tessellation.
- Distribute copies of Student Guide 25.1 and review the information provided with your students. Explain that they will use the figures on the data sheets to cover a surface, or plane—in this case, a sheet of construction paper. They will cut out the figures and use them to make their tessellations. Point out that they may need more than one copy of each data sheet. (At least two copies of each data sheet should be available for each student.)
- Hand out copies of Data Sheet 25.2: Triangles; Data Sheet 25.3: Quadrilaterals; and Data Sheet 25.4: Pentagons, Hexagons, and Octagons. Explain to your students that they can try using any of the figures on the data sheets to create their designs. They can use several figures if they wish; however, they must create a design that tessellates.
- Warn your students that not all of the figures on the data sheets will tessellate. Suggest that they experiment with arranging the figures on a sheet of paper to determine which ones will work.
- Instruct your students that after they have decided on their designs, they are to glue the figures onto construction paper. Encourage them to color the figures to highlight any patterns or symmetry in their tessellation.
- Remind your students that they are to write a brief description of their tessellation. They should use a separate sheet of paper that they can staple to the bottom of their tessellation. In their description they should include the names of the figures they used and any problems they encountered.

Wrap Up

Display your students' tessellations.

Extensions

Discuss why some figures tessellate and others do not. Ask your students to design multisided figures not found on the data sheets that will tessellate.

STUDENT GUIDE 25.1

Making a Tessellation

Project

You are to create a tessellation. You will make your tessellation using figures on Data Sheets 25.2, 25.3, and 25.4. You will also write a brief description of your tessellation.

Key Steps

1. A tessellation is a design formed by a repeating pattern of closed figures that covers a surface. This surface is called a plane. The figures must cover the surface completely. There can be no gaps or overlapping. Following is a design made of triangles that form a tessellation.

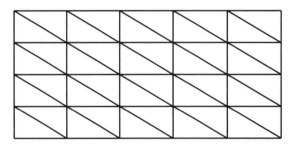

2. Study the shapes on the data sheets. Try to imagine which shapes will create a tessellation.

3. Carefully cut out the figures from the data sheets.

4. Arrange the figures on a piece of construction paper. Decide which ones will tessellate. Look for patterns. Try flipping, sliding, or rotating the figures to form an attractive design. Make sure there are no gaps or overlaps.

5. Glue the figures in place on the construction paper.

6. Color the figures. Coloring the patterns and symmetry will make your design special.

7. Write a brief description of your tessellation. Answer these questions: What figures did you use? Why did you choose these figures? What figures did you not use? What problems did you have making your tessellation?

Special Tip

- You can use more than one kind of figure in your tessellation. You do not have to use them all.

To Be Submitted

Your tessellation and its description

Triangles

Quadrilaterals

Pentagons, Hexagons, and Octagons

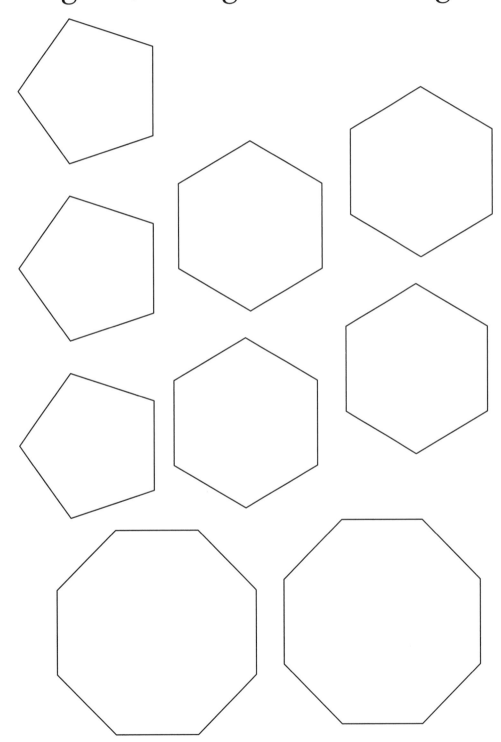

Making a Three-Dimensional Paper Sculpture from a Two-Dimensional Net

MOST STUDENTS ARE familiar with working with two-dimensional figures such as squares, rectangles, and triangles, which are usually described in terms of length and width or base and height. We live in a three-dimensional world, however, and the properties of three-dimensional figures include the added dimension of depth. Because students most often work with two-dimensional figures (at least in school), the concept, and certainly the visualization, of three-dimensional figures can cause confusion. In this project, students will make three-dimensional paper sculptures. As they complete their sculptures, they will become more familiar with the properties of three-dimensional figures.

Goal

Working individually, students will use nets to make a paper sculpture. The nets will be used to form cubes, tetrahedrons, and octahedrons. *Suggested time:* two to three class periods.

Skills Covered

1. Making a three-dimensional figure from a two-dimensional net
2. Identifying the terms *face, edge,* and *vertex*
3. Using visualization, spatial reasoning, and geometric modeling

Special Materials and Equipment

One 1-inch-by-3-inch-by-5-inch piece of Styrofoam for each student to use as the base of a sculpture, pipe cleaners (one for each figure in the sculpture each student will make), scissors, glue, markers, crayons, and colored pencils.

Development

- Before starting this project, make a sculpture of your own using a net. Show this sculpture to your students as an example. Also decide in advance which nets you will instruct your students to use. You may prefer that they work with only one, or you may allow them to work with two or all three. Another option is to allow your students to choose which nets they will construct. Younger students should probably be limited to one. Note that the cube is the easiest to construct and the octahedron is the most challenging.

- Begin this project by discussing with your students the difference between two-dimensional and three-dimensional figures. Show examples of some two-dimensional figures, such as squares and rectangles, on the board or a screen. Point out the dimensions, for example, length and width. Next show your students your example of a three-dimensional figure. Explain that it was created from a two-dimensional net that was folded and glued into its three-dimensional form. If necessary, explain that a net is a two-dimensional pattern that can be folded into a three-dimensional shape. Point out that the three-dimensional shape has length, width, and height. Also note its faces, edges, and vertices. Tell your students that they will make three-dimensional figures from two-dimensional nets.

- Distribute copies of Student Guide 26.1 and review the information it contains with your students. Go over the steps for creating their sculptures. If necessary, do some of the steps together as a class.

- Hand out copies of the data sheets your students will need: Data Sheet 26.2: Net for a Cube; Data Sheet 26.3: Net for a Tetrahedron; and Data Sheet 26.4: Net for an Octahedron. (Have extra copies of the nets available in the event that students make cutting mistakes.)

- Remind your students to cut along the solid lines and fold on the dotted lines of their nets. After folding on the dotted lines they should have formed a three-dimensional figure. If the figure does not have three dimensions, the student should double-check his or her steps and may need to start over.

- Show your students the faces, edges, and vertices of each figure. Note that the cube has 6 faces, 12 edges, and 8 vertices. The tetrahedron has 4 faces, 6 edges, and 4 vertices. The octahedron has 8 faces, 12 edges, and 6 vertices.

- Encourage your students to color the faces of their figures to make them more attractive. They should color the faces before they glue them together.

- Instruct your students that after they have glued together the faces of their figures, they are to attach their figures to their Styrofoam bases with pipe cleaners.

Math and Art

Wrap Up

Display the sculptures around the classroom. Review the properties of two-dimensional and three-dimensional figures.

Extension

Obtain nets of other platonic solids such as a dodecahedron or an icosahedron and encourage your students to make three-dimensional models of them.

Hands-On Math Projects

STUDENT GUIDE 26.1

Making a Three-Dimensional Paper Sculpture from a Two-Dimensional Net

Project

You will make a three-dimensional paper sculpture from a two-dimensional net. Your sculpture can be placed on any flat surface for display.

Key Steps

1. Your sculpture will be made from a two-dimensional drawing called a net.

2. Try to imagine how the net can form a three-dimensional figure.

3. Cut out the net along the solid lines.

4. Fold the net along the dotted lines.

5. Try to form a three-dimensional figure. If you cannot, check with your teacher. If necessary, start again with a new net.

6. If you wish to color the faces on your figure, flatten out the figure on your desk. It is now in two dimensions again. Color each outside face.

7. Refold your figure. It should now be in three dimensions.

8. Glue together the flaps.

9. Place the Styrofoam base on your desk.

10. Insert one end of a pipe cleaner into one vertex (corner) of your figure. Place the other end of the pipe cleaner into the Styrofoam. If you have other figures, attach them to the base in the same way.

Special Tips

- Be sure not to cut on the dotted lines.
- Be sure you are drawing on the outside faces of the figure, not the inside.

To Be Submitted

Your sculpture

Net for a Cube

Net for a Tetrahedron

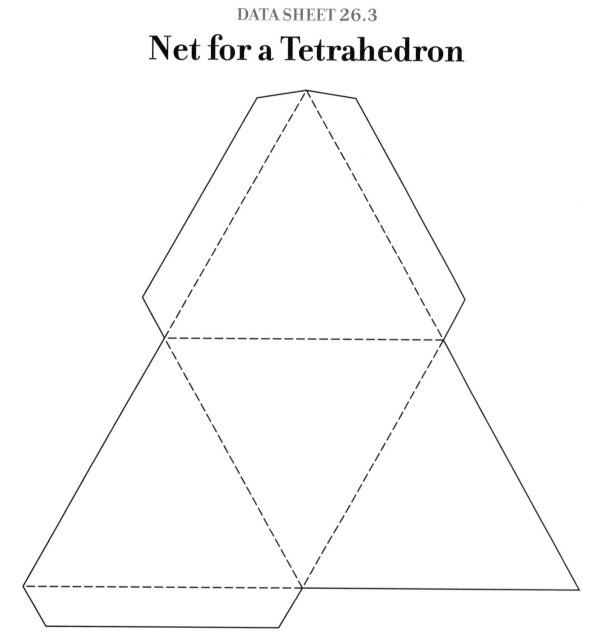

Net for an Octahedron

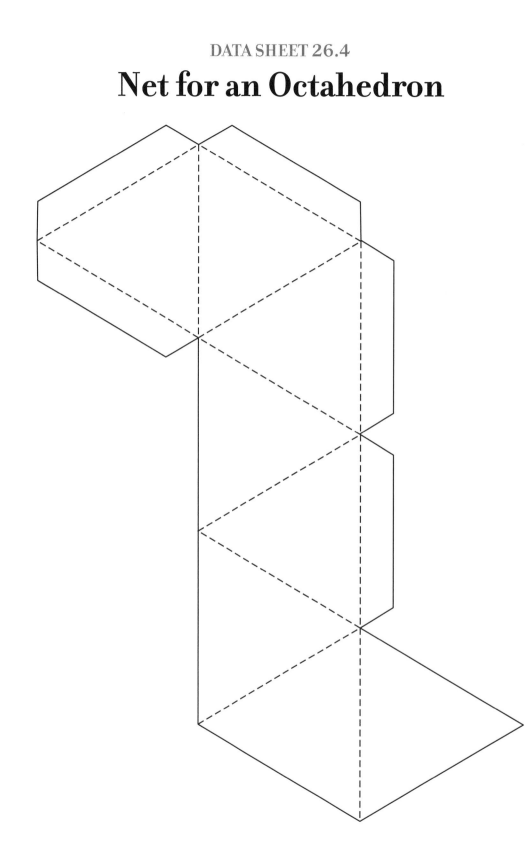

Chapter Eight

Math and Recreation

The Math in a Favorite Sport

MOST STUDENTS ENJOY PARTICIPATING in or watching sports. Few, however, ever consider the importance of math to sports. Standardized playing surfaces, rules, and scoring are based on numbers. For this project, your students have the chance to examine a favorite sport in a fresh way—from the perspective of numbers.

Goal

Working in groups of three or four, students are to select a favorite sport and describe it in terms of math. They will make an oral presentation of their findings to the class. They will also support their findings with charts, tables, or illustrations. *Suggested time:* three to four class periods.

Skills Covered

1. Researching the mathematical aspects of a specific sport
2. Creating tables, charts, or diagrams
3. Measuring and using a scale
4. Using math to communicate ideas
5. Using technology (if computers are used)

Special Materials and Equipment

Reference books, including encyclopedias and resources on sports; poster paper; rulers; index cards; markers, crayons, colored pencils, and felt-tipped pens. Optional: computers with Internet access.

Development

- Before beginning this project, ask your school's librarian to set aside reference books that your students can use in researching their topics, especially encyclopedias, which will provide basic information about major sports, and books on particular sports. You may also wish to reserve a period in the library for your students to conduct their research.

- Start the project by asking your students if they enjoy sports. A show of hands will likely indicate that most do. Explain that mathematics plays a major role in every sport. Ask your students to think of ways that math is important to their favorite sport. For example, keeping score, the dimensions of playing surfaces, size of equipment, game periods, and penalties are all based on math.

- Explain that for this project students will work in groups of three or four. They will choose a favorite sport and describe the ways in which math is important to the game. Explain that they will present their findings to the class in an oral report, and they will support their findings with tables, charts, or diagrams.

- Distribute copies of Student Guide 27.1 and review the information provided with your students. Note that although they may select any sport for this project, major sports such as baseball, football, soccer, basketball, hockey, and tennis will be easier to research. These sports also rely heavily on math.

- Depending on the abilities of your students and their access to computers, encourage them to check Web sites for information. Search terms such as *baseball*, *football*, and *soccer* will result in numerous sites. Mention that the Web sites of professional leagues and sports associations are likely to contain the most useful information. Also, note that some Web sites may have so much information that students will have to look closely and carefully for the information they need.

- Hand out copies of Data Sheet 27.2: Sports and Math, which lists some ways that math is important to sports. Note that the list offers only guidelines; some sports may rely on math in ways other than what is presented on the data sheet.

- After your students have gathered their data, they are to organize it. Suggest that they write notes on index cards, to which they may refer during their presentations.

- Remind your students that they must also illustrate some aspect of their findings. They may create a chart, table, or a diagram. If they choose to make a diagram of a field or court, they should provide the dimensions, show any special areas, and provide a key if necessary. Depending on the abilities of your students, encourage them to draw their diagram to scale.

- Suggest that each group choose a spokesperson or spokespersons to present the group's findings to the class.

Wrap Up

Have your students make their presentations to the class. Display their charts, tables, and diagrams.

Extension

Encourage your students to compare the statistics of some of the top players in a sport of their choice. Point out that statistics are a special branch of mathematics.

Copyright © 2009 by Judith A. and Gary Robert Muschla

STUDENT GUIDE 27.1

The Math in a Favorite Sport

Project

Your group will choose a favorite sport. You will find ways that math is important to this sport. You will then present your findings to the class. You will support your data with a table, chart, or diagram.

Key Steps

1. Decide which sport your group would like to research.

2. Brainstorm and list ways that math is important to your sport. Use the topics on Data Sheet 27.2 as a guide.

3. Organize your data.

4. To prepare for your presentation, write important facts on index cards. The cards will help you to remember important information.

5. Create a table, chart, or diagram to illustrate your data. You might make a chart showing the ways that math is important to your sport. You might draw a diagram that shows a playing field. Include the dimensions on any diagram. Also include any special areas of a field or court. If possible, draw your diagram according to a scale.

6. Decide who will present your findings to the class.

Special Tips

• Gather information from different sources.

• Divide the tasks of research among the group's members. Have each member find information about a different idea. This will make the overall task of researching easier.

To Be Submitted

Your index cards and chart, table, or diagram

DATA SHEET 27.2

Sports and Math

Math plays a big part in most sports. Following are some of the ways in which math is important to sports. There are other ways.

1. Size of a field, court, or other playing surface
2. Parts or divisions of playing areas
3. Number of players on a team
4. Number of positions on a team
5. Size of goals or nets
6. Size (length, width, weight) of equipment
7. Size and weight of ball or puck
8. Time of game
9. Division of time for game
10. Scorekeeping
11. Ways that numbers are used in the rules
12. Noteworthy records

Notes:

_____

_____

_____

_____

_____

_____

_____

_____

_____

_____

Inventing a Math Board Game

MOST STUDENTS LOVE TO PLAY GAMES. Some would no doubt prefer to play a game rather than learn math (or any other subject). In this project, students can combine designing and playing a game with learning about math.

Goal

Working in groups of three or four, students will create a board game about math. *Suggested time:* four to five class periods.

Skills Covered

1. Various math skills according to the content of the games that students create

2. Using visualization and spatial relationships to design the game board

3. Using measurement to design and construct the game board

4. Writing as a means to express ideas about math

5. Using technology (if calculators are used)

Special Materials and Equipment

Heavy poster paper, graph paper, assorted colors of construction paper, and 4-inch-by-6-inch index cards; scissors, rulers, markers, crayons, felt-tipped pens, colored pencils, and glue. Optional: calculators.

Development

- To keep this project manageable and to provide your students with direction, consider the following example of a board game that students may create:

Players must travel thirty spaces to reach a destination: Top Math Student. The spaces cover the playing surface of the board. For each turn, students pick a card from a set of cards placed on the game board. Each card contains a math problem that the player must solve. The problems are labeled with degree of difficulty. If students choose a card with an easy problem and solve the problem correctly, they move two spaces forward on the board. If they choose a card with a problem of average difficulty and answer correctly, they move four spaces forward. If they choose a card with a challenging problem and answer correctly, they move six spaces forward. If they answer incorrectly, they move the same number of spaces backward or stay on the same space if they are at the beginning of the game. Along the way certain spaces on the board denote hazards (perhaps a player landing on such a space "catches a cold" and loses a turn) or bonuses (for example, the player is recognized as student of the month and moves an extra space forward). The inclusion of hazard and bonus spaces adds to the element of chance in the game. The winner of the game is the student who finishes first.

- Because math is central to this kind of game, before beginning the project you should consider whether you will limit students to specific topics—perhaps the current unit of study—or allow them to use a broad range of topics and skills. You might, for example, permit them to use material from all of the skills they have mastered so far in math.
- Introduce this project by discussing with your students the different kinds of board games they have played. Point out that many board games involve traveling around a board to reach a destination. Players may use a spinner, roll dice, or pick a card to determine each move.
- Begin the project by explaining to your students that they will work in groups to create a math board game. Share with them a summary of the sample game described earlier and encourage them to use it as a guide for the game they create. Creative students will easily expand on the concept. However, if students have trouble coming up with a game, allow them to use the example for their game.
- Note that math must be a central part of the game. Students can pick cards with math questions and problems on them that they must answer correctly in order to move along the board, as in the example presented; or they must think of

another way to use math in the game. This will ensure that math is an important component.

- Hand out copies of Student Guide 28.1 and review the information provided with your students. Note whether you want them to focus on specific topics or choose from varied material they have learned.

- Distribute copies of Data Sheet 28.2: Guidelines for Creating a Math Board Game. Discuss with your students the information it provides. Note that not all of the guidelines may apply to the particular game they create.

- Encourage your students to plan their game before attempting to create their game board. They should decide on the game's rules and on how a player wins. They should then make a rough sketch of the game on graph paper.

- Explain to your students that after they have revised their sketch they can begin making their game board on heavy poster paper. Caution them to use rulers for measuring and drawing straight lines. Suggest that they draw any lines lightly in pencil first and then, after they are certain that the lines are where they want them to be, go over them with markers or felt-tipped pens.

- Emphasize to your students that all the math they use must be correct. Remind them to double-check the answers to any problems. You may want to suggest that they check their computation with calculators. They should keep an answer key on a separate sheet of paper. Before they complete their games, you should check their cards and answer keys for content and accuracy.

- Encourage your students to decorate their game board with illustrations.

Wrap Up

After checking the games, allow the groups to play each other's games.

Extension

Encourage your students to update their games with new or more challenging problems.

Name _____   Date _____

STUDENT GUIDE 28.1

Inventing a Math Board Game

Project

Your group will create a math board game.

Key Steps

1. Think about different board games you have played. How were they designed? What were their rules? How did a player move along the board? How did a player win?

2. Brainstorm and list ideas for your math board game. Choose your favorite.

3. Decide how many players can play your game at the same time.

4. Write a rough draft of the rules for your game. You must understand your game before you can make your game board. For example, you must answer such questions as the following:

   - How many spaces must players travel to win?
   - How many cards with math questions or problems will be needed?
   - How many spaces forward will a player move with a correct answer?
   - How many spaces backward will a player move with an incorrect answer?
   - How many, if any, hazards will your game have? What will the hazards be?
   - How many, if any, bonuses will your game have? What will the bonuses be?

   See Data Sheet 28.2 for additional guidelines.

5. Sketch a rough copy of your game board on graph paper. Estimate distances and try to place things where they will be on the actual board.

6. Double-check your sketch. Make any revisions you feel are needed.

7. Draw your game board on heavy poster paper. Be neat and draw lightly in pencil first. Use rulers to measure lengths and to make straight lines.

8. Use a felt-tipped pen or fine marker for permanent lines.

9. Make any game cards you need for your game. Estimate how many you will need for one complete game.

10. Make playing pieces for your game.

11. Make a final copy of the rules for your game.

12. On a separate sheet of paper make an answer key for the math problems in your game. Be sure the answers to all problems are correct.

Inventing a Math Board Game *(Cont'd.)*

Special Tips

- Use rulers to draw straight lines and spaces.
- To make game cards, start with 4-inch-by-6-inch index cards. Measure and cut the cards in half lengthwise. This will make cards that are 4 inches long and 3 inches wide. Write a math question or problem on one side of each card. Also write the number of spaces a player will move forward with a correct answer (or backward with an incorrect answer). Try to make an even mix of easy, average, and hard problems. Players should move forward more spaces by solving hard problems. Number each card in the lower left corner. The numbers will help you make an accurate answer key.
- Here is a way to make game pieces. Take an index card and cut 1-inch-by-2-inch strips. Fold the strips in half so that you have two 1-inch squares. Bend one side up so that it is at a right angle to the base. It should stand up straight. Make a game piece for each player. Choose a different color for each game piece.
- Make your game board interesting and attractive by adding colorful illustrations.

To Be Submitted

Your game board, game cards, playing pieces, a list of rules, and an answer key

DATA SHEET 28.2

Guidelines for Creating a Math Board Game

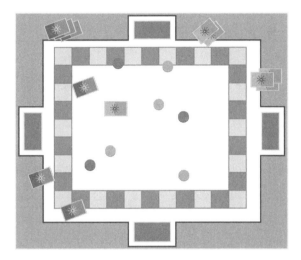

1. Decide how many spaces players must travel to win. Between 24 and 36 spaces will work well for most games.

2. Decide if there will be special spaces on your board. What will they be? Where will they be?

3. Decide how big (long and wide) your spaces will be. A good size is 2 inches by 3 inches. Use a ruler to estimate the path of the spaces. Make sure you will not run out of room. For example, if one space is 3 inches long, you will need a game board that is 30 inches long to fit 10 spaces in a straight row. If you want to leave a 1-inch margin around your board, you will be able to fit only 9 spaces. Measuring is very important.

4. Design your game cards and game pieces.

5. Mark a spot for placing the game cards.

6. Include labels such as *start* and *end*.

7. Write a set of rules for your game.

8. Draw and color pictures on your game board to make it interesting.

9. Write the name of the game at the top of the board.

Creating Math Puzzles

MOST STUDENTS ENJOY THE CHALLENGE of solving puzzles. An even greater challenge is to create puzzles for other students to solve. To design an interesting math puzzle, students must possess mastery over the skills required to solve the puzzle. Thus, math puzzles are a fine learning experience for both the puzzle creators and the puzzle solvers.

Goal

Working in pairs or groups of three, students will create a cross number puzzle or a magic square for other students to solve. *Suggested time:* two to three class periods.

Skills Covered

1. Various math skills depending on the content of the puzzles that students create

2. Using technology (if computers or calculators are used)

Special Materials and Equipment

Graph paper, rulers, correction fluid, and black pens or fine-point markers. Optional: computers with Internet access and calculators.

Development

- Prior to beginning this project, gather examples of cross number puzzles and magic squares. Although you may limit your students to the puzzles described in this project, you may also expand the project and allow them to create other kinds of puzzles, including math word scrambles, math rebuses, coded messages, and Sudoku puzzles. Examples of puzzles can be found in math resource books as well as on the Internet. Searching on terms such as *math puzzles* or the specific name of a puzzle such as *magic squares* will lead to numerous Web sites. Review any Web sites before directing students to them to make certain that the Web sites offer puzzles that are appropriate for the abilities of your students.

- Also before beginning the project, decide if you want your students to focus on specific topics—for example, fractions—or on a particular operation—such as division—or if you will allow them to create puzzles on a wide variety of math topics and skills.

- Begin this project by explaining to your students that they will work in pairs or in groups of three to create math puzzles. Tell them that upon completion of the project, the puzzles will be photocopied and they will try to solve one another's puzzles.

- Mention whether your students are to concentrate on specific topics, such as your current unit of study, or have the freedom to choose from a variety of material.

- Hand out copies of Student Guide 29.1 and review the information it provides with your students. Note that they should use graph paper for creating magic squares and cross number puzzles. Suggest that they try to design a three-by-three magic square (which has a total of nine squares). Encourage them to attempt larger magic squares, but note that the more squares a magic square has, the more challenging the puzzle becomes. For cross number puzzles, suggest that they design puzzles with three or four problems down and three or four across. Again, encourage them to attempt bigger puzzles, but the more problems the puzzle has, the more complicated it will be.

- Distribute copies of Data Sheet 29.2: Sample Math Puzzles, which contains an example of a cross number puzzle and a magic square. Discuss the examples with your students, being sure to point out the features of each puzzle.

- Depending on the abilities of your students and their access to computers, encourage them to visit Web sites to study additional examples of puzzles. Remind them to study the puzzles and not spend too much time trying to solve them.

- Instruct your students to create rough copies of their puzzles first. Only after making certain the puzzles are accurate should they complete final copies.

- You may also suggest that your students create their puzzles on a computer. Most word processing software allows users to easily create the grids for magic squares or cross number puzzles. In Microsoft Word, for example, you can create grids by clicking on the Table button on the tool bar. However, this can be challenging for young students.

- Remind your students that all of the math in their puzzles must be correct. If you wish, you may allow them to double-check their work with calculators.

- Instruct your students to create answer keys for their puzzles.

Wrap Up

Make copies of your students' puzzles and allow them to solve the puzzles of their classmates.

Extensions

Encourage your students to explore other types of math puzzles, some of which they may create.

You might also compile a class math puzzle book.

Name _____   Date _____

Creating Math Puzzles

Project

You and your partner or group will create a math puzzle that other students will try to solve.

Key Steps

1. Study the sample math puzzles on Data Sheet 29.2. If possible, check Web sites on the Internet for other examples. Search by using *magic squares, cross number puzzles,* or *math puzzles for students*.

2. Decide on the type of puzzle you want to create.

3. Decide on the topic of your puzzle. You may do a cross number puzzle on addition of whole numbers. You may do one on multiplication. You may also do one on all four operations. You can even do one on fractions or decimals.

4. Create the problems you will use in your puzzle. Make sure your math is correct.

5. Make a rough copy of your puzzle on graph paper. For a magic square, start with a puzzle of nine squares. For a cross number puzzle, start with three or four problems down and three or four across. Expand your puzzle, if possible, by adding more problems.

6. Carefully double-check your rough copy. Make sure your puzzle is correct.

7. Use graph paper for your final copy. Use a ruler and a fine-point black marker or pen to draw the boxes. Do not make any unnecessary marks on your puzzle.

8. Create an answer key for your puzzle.

Special Tip

• Double-check your puzzle and answer key before handing them in to your teacher.

To Be Submitted

The final copy of your puzzle and your answer key

DATA SHEET 29.2

Sample Math Puzzles

Cross number puzzle: A cross number puzzle is like a crossword puzzle with numbers. The answers to the problems are written on the puzzles. One digit is placed in each box. In the following puzzle, numbers 2 and 3 down and numbers 1 and 6 across are done for you.

Solution

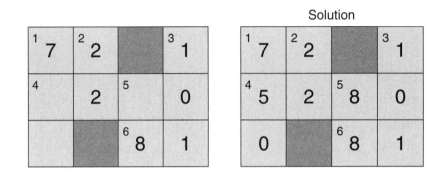

Down

1. 75×10

2. $30 - 8$

3. $15 + 37 + 49$

5. 8×11

Across

1. 18×4

4. The number of feet in a mile

6. 9×9

Magic square: In a magic square, the sum of the numbers in each column, row, and diagonal is the same. You must find the missing numbers. In the following magic square, the sum of the numbers in each column, row, and diagonal is 15.

Solution

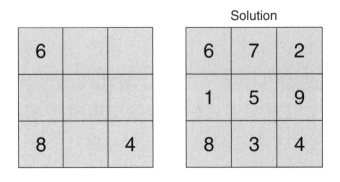

Exploring Math Web Sites

IF YOUR STUDENTS are like most, they have little trouble finding Web sites for music, games, and sports. However, they may not fully understand the Internet's enormous capacity as a resource for information. By encouraging your students to explore math Web sites, this project will help them gain a glimpse of the Internet's vast scope. It may even stimulate their interest in math when they see how much fun some math Web sites can be.

Goal

Working in pairs or groups of three, students will visit various math Web sites. They will choose a favorite Web site and write a description of it. They will then share their favorite Web site with the class during a discussion. *Suggested time:* two to three class periods.

Skills Covered

1. Gathering, analyzing, and organizing information
2. Making decisions on the basis of data
3. Writing as a means of communicating ideas about mathematics
4. Using technology

Special Materials and Equipment

Computers with Internet access.

Development

• Ask your students about Web sites they have visited. Discuss what factors help to make one Web site better than another. Ask for volunteers to describe any math Web sites they have visited. Consider these questions: Does the Web site offer information about math? Does it offer games and puzzles? What makes the Web site interesting?

• Begin this project by explaining to your students that they will work in pairs or groups of three. They are to visit math Web sites and choose a favorite, then write a brief description of it, stating the reasons why they chose it. Upon completion of the project, students will share their favorite math Web sites during a class discussion.

• Hand out copies of Student Guide 30.1 and review the information on it with your students. Note that they should visit at least three math Web sites, or more if they have time. One way to find math Web sites is by going to http://kids.yahoo.com, clicking on Studyzone, and then clicking on math. They may find additional Web sites by using any major search engine and searching on *math Web sites for students*.

• Distribute copies of Worksheet 30.2: Math Web Sites. Note that the worksheet provides space for students to record their impressions about math Web sites. Explain that they are to write down the name of the Web site, its URL (Uniform Resource Locator, which is the site's address), and what they like or dislike about the Web site. They should use extra sheets of paper if necessary. The information they record on their worksheets will be the basis of their written descriptions.

• If your school has a computer room with Internet access, reserve time there for your students. While students are online, be sure to circulate, answer any questions they may have, and keep them on task. (Computer-savvy kids can visit a lot of Web sites other than math in a short time.)

• Remind your students that after they have chosen a favorite math Web site they are to write a description of it. Encourage them to use an opening, body, and conclusion in their writing. They should support their main ideas with details. Emphasize too that they should review and revise their writing.

Wrap Up

Conduct a class discussion in which students share their favorite math Web sites. Encourage them to give the reasons they chose those Web sites. Display the written descriptions of Web sites on bulletin boards.

Extension

Encourage your students to visit some of the favorite math Web sites of their classmates.

Copyright © 2009 by Judith A. and Gary Robert Muschla

STUDENT GUIDE 30.1

Exploring Math Web Sites

Project

You and your partner or group are to choose a favorite math Web site. You should visit three to five (or more) Web sites before choosing your favorite. You will write a description of your favorite math Web site. Finally, you will share your choice with the class during a discussion.

Key Steps

1. Visit math Web sites. You can find these by searching on *math Web sites for students*. You can also visit http://kids.yahoo.com. Click on Studyzone and then click on math.

2. When visiting math Web sites, ask yourself the following questions:
   - Is the Web site easy to use?
   - Does it have interesting or useful information?
   - Does it offer games or puzzles?
   - How is it different from other math Web sites?
   - Is it helpful to you as a math student?

3. Discuss with your partner or group what you like or dislike about each Web site.

4. Complete Worksheet 30.2. It will help you record your thoughts about each Web site.

5. Working with your partner or group, pick a favorite Web site. List your reasons for choosing it as your favorite.

6. Write a description of your favorite math Web site. Include an opening, body, and conclusion in your writing. Use your notes from Worksheet 30.2 for ideas. Tell why this is your favorite Web site. Be sure to support your main ideas with details. Revise your writing.

7. Prepare to discuss your favorite math Web site with the class.

Special Tips

- Make sure the Web sites you visit are for students your age. Do not spend time on Web sites for older students.
- Many Web sites have links to other Web sites. Explore these links in your search for a favorite math Web site.

To Be Submitted

Your written description

WORKSHEET 30.2

Math Web Sites

Write notes about the math Web sites you visit. Use additional sheets of paper if necessary.

1. Name of Web site: _____ URL: _____

What I like about this Web site: _____

_____

_____

What I dislike about this Web site: _____

_____

_____

2. Name of Web site: _____ URL: _____

What I like about this Web site: _____

_____

_____

What I dislike about this Web site: _____

_____

_____

3. Name of Web site: _____ URL: _____

What I like about this Web site: _____

_____

_____

What I dislike about this Web site: _____

_____

_____

The Math in Planning a Birthday Party

BY THE TIME THEY ENTER SCHOOL, most students have gone to plenty of birthday parties. Few are aware of the time and thought spent in planning a party, and even fewer are aware of the costs, which can be significant. In this project, your students will explore the essentials of party planning.

Goal

Working in groups of three or four, students are to imagine that they are planning a birthday party for a friend. They are to choose the foods and items necessary for the party, and calculate the total cost. At the end of the project they will describe their party plan to the class. *Suggested time:* two to three class periods.

Skills Covered

1. Making decisions on the basis of data
2. Estimating costs
3. Addition with decimals
4. Multiplication with decimals
5. Comparing sizes
6. Calculating total costs
7. Using technology (if calculators or computers are used)

Special Materials and Equipment

Optional: calculators, grocery store circulars containing the prices of foods and other items that might be used for a party, computers with Internet access because some grocery stores make their circulars available online.

Development

- To broaden the scope of this project, you may wish to collect grocery store circulars in advance. Although Data Sheet 31.2: Birthday Party Basics contains the foods, items, and prices your students will need to complete the project, circulars can provide students with more choices. They will also give students a chance to work with a common form of advertisement and select relevant items from a wide variety of possibilities.

- Start this project by explaining to your students that they will work in groups. They are to imagine that they are to plan a birthday party for a friend. They are to pick all of the foods and items they believe necessary for an outstanding party, including the cake, ice cream, chips and pretzels, and necessities such as paper plates, napkins, candles, and decorations.

- Distribute copies of Student Guide 31.1 and review the information it contains with your students. Explain that they are to assume that twelve people will attend the party. They should plan the best party they can while limiting costs as much as possible. At the end of the project have students vote for what they feel is the best party at the lowest cost. This will help promote both frugality and quality.

- Hand out copies of Data Sheet 31.2. Explain that the data sheet contains a variety of foods and items commonly found at birthday parties. Note that prices are included, and that for some items the prices are shown for two sizes. Students should decide which size would be best for their party. Make sure they understand that a serving size is the recommended amount of a food an average person consumes at one time. Point out the decimal values for the amounts of some items. If necessary, discuss with your students how much these amounts represent. For example, ice cream is commonly packaged in 1.75-quart containers; this is the ice cream container size that most students will find in their freezer at home. Caution your students that although they should try to avoid waste, they also do not want to run out of anything. Note that they do not have to select every type of food and item on the data sheet.

- If you hand out grocery store circulars to your students, explain that they may choose items from the circulars as well as the data sheet. Obviously, however, not all items in the circulars will apply to a birthday party. Students should read the circulars carefully.

- Depending on the abilities of your students and their access to computers, you may suggest that they check online grocery store circulars as well. (Be sure to check the Web sites of grocery stores in advance to make sure that circulars are available and that the Web site is easy enough for students to navigate.)

- Suggest that your students estimate costs as they go along. Review estimation with them if necessary.
- Hand out copies of Worksheet 31.3: Birthday Party Cost and Tally Sheet. Make sure your students understand each of the columns. Instruct them to complete the worksheet by listing the foods and items they choose for their party as well as the prices. You may permit them to use calculators in tallying their costs.
- Note that your students should choose a spokesperson to describe their group's birthday party choices to the class. They may find it helpful to refer to their completed worksheet as they make their presentations.

Wrap Up

Students share their birthday party plans with the class. Discuss the different choices the groups made. Vote for the best party at the lowest cost.

Extension

If your class has a holiday or an end-of-the-year party, allow the students to help plan it. Use math in planning the party, and stay within a budget.

Name _____   Date _____

The Math in Planning a Birthday Party

Project

Your group is to imagine that it is planning a birthday party for a friend. Twelve people will attend the party. You will choose all of the foods and supplies you will need. You will then find the total cost for the party. At the end of the project, you will describe your party plan to the class. The class will vote for the best party at the lowest price.

Key Steps

1. Think about birthday parties you have gone to. Discuss with your group the kinds of foods and supplies (paper plates, cups, streamers, and so on) that are at birthday parties.

2. Make a list of foods and supplies you want for your party.

3. Estimate the amounts of food you will need for twelve people. Pay close attention to serving sizes. Try not to buy more than you will need. Remember that some people may want extra servings of some foods.

4. Keep a running list of the costs of the foods and materials. If you feel you are spending too much money, eliminate some things.

5. Complete Worksheet 31.3. Write down all of the foods and supplies and their prices. Find the total cost for your party.

6. Choose a spokesperson to share your party plan with the class.

Special Tip

- Think of ways you can save money. For example, you may buy plastic cups for serving soda, juice, and water. This can reduce how much is served. Letting people drink from cans or bottles eliminates the need for cups. But this means that each person will need a can or a bottle of his or her own.

To Be Submitted

Your completed worksheet

DATA SHEET 31.2

Birthday Party Basics

Food

Cake

8-inch round, $10.99, serves 8–12 people

10-inch round, $16.99, serves 12–15 people

Ice Cream

1 pint of chocolate or vanilla or strawberry, $2.49, 4 half-cup servings

1 pint of chocolate, vanilla, and strawberry, $2.49, 4 half-cup servings

1.75 quarts of chocolate or vanilla or strawberry, $4.69, 14 half-cup servings

1.75 quarts of chocolate, vanilla, and strawberry, $4.69, 14 half-cup servings

Beverages

Soda

    2-liter bottle of cola, $1.59, 8 one-cup servings

    1 12-pack (12-ounce cans) of cola, $4.49, 12 servings

Apple juice

    0.5-gallon container of apple juice, $2.99, 8 one-cup servings

    1 8-pack (6.75-fluid-ounce cans), $3.39, 8 servings

Water

    1 12-pack (0.5-liter bottles) of spring water, $4.29, 12 servings

Snacks

Pretzels

    1 package (16 ounces), $2.79, serves 16 people

Potato chips

    1 package (13 ounces), $3.49, serves 13 people

Materials

Plastic plates, 15 for $1.69   Plastic table cloth, $1.29

Plastic bowls, 18 for $2.69   Plastic cups, 30 for $0.99

Plastic spoons, 24 for $1.39   Streamers, $0.99 per roll

Plastic forks, 24 for $1.39   Candles, 24 for $1.49

Napkins, 120 for $0.99   Balloons, 10 for $1.59

Birthday Party Cost and Tally Sheet

Item	How Many?	Cost for Each	Total

Total Cost _____

Chapter Nine

Math and Life Skills

Measuring Up in Metric and Customary Units

ALTHOUGH THE METRIC SYSTEM is slowly becoming more common in the United States, most students continue to rely on customary units for measurement. In measuring length, for example, inches, feet, and yards hold more meaning for most Americans than do millimeters, centimeters, and meters. In this project, students will estimate and measure the lengths of a variety of objects in class, giving them a chance to work with both metric and customary units.

Goal

Working in pairs or groups of three, students will estimate, then measure the length of at least ten objects in the classroom. They will choose the most appropriate unit in both metric and customary systems. *Suggested time:* one to two class periods.

Skills Covered

1. Estimating length in metric and customary units
2. Measuring length in metric and customary units
3. Selecting the most appropriate unit of measure

Special Materials and Equipment

For each pair or group of students, two standard rulers with two scales, one in millimeters and centimeters, the other in inches and feet; paper clips. Optional: yardsticks and metersticks.

Development

- Discuss with your students both the metric and the customary systems of measuring length. The customary system, also known as the English system, developed in England over many centuries. At one time, the *foot* was based on the length of a king's actual foot. When a new king came to power, so did a new measurement for the foot. The metric system was developed in France in 1789. It is officially known as the International System of Units. Unlike the customary system, in which there is little consistency in finding equivalent values of measurement (12 inches = 1 foot but 3 feet = 1 yard), the metric system is based on powers of ten (1 meter = 10 decimeters = 100 centimeters = 1000 millimeters) and 1 millimeter = 1/1000 meter; 1 centimeter = 1/100 meter; and 1 decimeter = 1/10 meter.

- Because the metric system is based on powers of ten, many people believe that once this system is learned, metric units are easier to use than customary units. The United States is slowly adopting metric measurement. Point out to your students that most packages now come with weights or volumes expressed in both metric and customary units. You might also mention that the metric system is commonly used in science throughout the world.

- Start this project by explaining to your students that they will work in pairs or in groups of three. They will first estimate the length of common objects in the classroom in both metric and customary units, then they will actually measure the objects. They are to choose the most appropriate unit of length for each object.

- Provide some examples of using appropriate units. You might use the length of a bookcase and a tile on the floor as examples. Ask your students which metric and customary units to use for measuring these objects. A long bookcase might best be measured in meters or feet; a smaller one, in centimeters or inches. Millimeters are too small in either case, although yards could be used to measure a long bookcase. A floor tile would probably best be measured in centimeters or inches, unless the tile is 12 inches long, in which case it should be measured as one foot. Again, millimeters would not be appropriate.

- Distribute copies of Student Guide 32.1 and review the information it provides with your students. If necessary, demonstrate how to measure length in millimeters, centimeters, and meters, and in inches, feet, and yards. Caution students to measure accurately. Note that the scale of some rulers does not start at the beginning of the ruler. Students must start to measure where the scale begins.

- Hand out copies of Worksheet 32.2: Measure This. The worksheet contains five classroom objects that your students must measure. They are also to measure five other objects of their choice; however, you may encourage them to measure more than five. You might want to suggest objects for them to measure as well as objects that you prefer them not to measure. For example, anything that requires students to stand on chairs or desks should not be permitted. (They can come up with some truly astonishing objects to measures.) Review the worksheet with them, noting the spaces for estimates and actual measurements. If necessary, review the abbreviations for meters, centimeters, millimeters, yards, feet, and inches. Remind your students that they are to use the most appropriate, or best, unit of measure for each object.

Wrap Up

Discuss with your students the differences between metric and customary units of measurement for length. Which did they find to be easier to use? Why?

Extension

Have students measure the mass and volume of other objects in both metric and customary units.

Name _____   Date _____

Measuring Up in Metric and Customary Units

Project

You and your partner or group are to measure the lengths of objects in your classroom. You will estimate the lengths in both metric and customary units. Then you will find the actual lengths.

Key Steps

1. Make sure you understand how to measure length in both metric and customary units.

2. Keep in mind the basic units of measurement for length in customary units:
   - 1 foot = 12 inches
   - 1 yard = 3 feet = 36 inches

3. Remember the basic units of measurement for length in the metric system:

   1 meter = 100 centimeters = 1000 millimeters

4. Complete Worksheet 32.2. Choose the best measuring unit in both metric and customary systems. Estimate the length of the object, then find its actual length. Measure the five objects on the worksheet. Next, measure five objects of your choice. Remember to compare your estimates with the actual lengths. Be sure to measure accurately.

Special Tips

- To measure the length of an object, place the beginning of the ruler's scale at one end of the object. Measure the distance to the other end. Note that the beginning of the ruler's scale may not be at the beginning of the ruler.

- If your ruler is shorter than the total length of the object you are measuring, measure the length in stages. Start at the end of the object and measure to the end of the ruler. If you have another ruler, place the beginning of the scale of the second ruler at the end of the scale of the first. Now move the first ruler to the end of the second. Repeat the process as many times as necessary. Be sure to total the lengths.

To Be Submitted

Your completed worksheet

Name _____   Date _____

Measure This

Estimate the length of each of the following items. Write your estimate in the best metric and customary units. Then measure the object. Write the measurement in the best metric and customary units. Next, estimate and measure 5 objects of your own. Write the measurement in the best metric and customary units.

Things to Measure		Metric Units (m, cm, or mm)		Customary Units (yd, ft, or in.)	
		Estimate	Actual	Estimate	Actual
1.	Length of this paper				
2.	Length of a pencil				
3.	Length of a student's arm				
4.	Width of a paper clip				
5.	Height of a student				
6.					
7.					
8.					
9.					
10.					

Buying Books for the School Library

MAKING ANY KIND OF LARGE PURCHASE involves careful thought and math skills. This project not only gives your students practice in adding and subtracting money, but it also promotes research, evaluation, and decision-making skills. Moreover, it introduces your students to popular books. On completion of the project, your students may wish to recommend that some of these books be purchased for their school's library.

Goal

Working in groups of three or four, students are to select books for the school library. They will be given a list of books and prices and are to imagine they have a budget of $100. Upon conclusion of the project, they will present their results to the class. *Suggested time:* two to three class periods.

Skills Covered

1. Estimating costs and planning within a budget
2. Evaluating data to make decisions
3. Adding and subtracting money
4. Using mathematics to communicate ideas
5. Using technology (if calculators or computers are used)

Special Materials and Equipment

Optional: calculators, computers with Internet access, book lists, and a variety of novels that students may review and evaluate.

Development

- You have several options regarding the book lists that are necessary for this project. You may of course simply have your students use Data Sheet 33.2: Book List, which lists books and their prices that students can use to complete the project. The list contains twenty popular novels for students in grades 3 to 5. Many of these books may already be in your school library. An option you may prefer is to create your own data sheet listing books that you like or that you use in class. You can easily find the prices of these books on the Web site of any number of online booksellers. You may also use book catalogs aimed at students, or perhaps your librarian has old catalogs that your students might use. Whichever book list you use, try to obtain copies of some of the books in advance. Allowing students to see and examine the books will stimulate their interest and help them in making their selections. They may even decide to read some of the books—an added bonus for sure. After you have decided how you will present the books from which students are to make their selections, you are ready to begin the project.

- Start by explaining to your students that librarians set aside money each year for buying new books and for replacing books that have worn out or been lost. This money is part of a library's overall budget. If necessary, explain that a budget is a plan for controlling how much money a person spends.

- Tell your students to imagine that the class has been given $100 with which to buy books for the school library. The class will be divided into groups, and each group will choose books they feel the library should have.

- Hand out copies of Student Guide 33.1 and review the information on it with your students. Call attention to the various factors they should consider when deciding which books to buy. For example, they should aim for a balance of books, such as those that will likely interest both boys and girls, those that will appeal to multiple reading grade levels, and both hardcover and paperback editions. Emphasize to your students that they should estimate costs as they go along. This will help them to stay within their budgets.

- Distribute copies of Data Sheet 33.2, or distribute copies of a book list or catalog of your own. Explain to your students that these are the books from which they are to choose. (You may also open up the project and permit your students to recommend books that are not on the list. In this case, they will need to find the prices of the hardcover and paperback editions themselves.) Suggest that group members discuss with one another the books the group is considering. Encourage those students who might have read some of the books to share their opinions with the other group members.

- If you have sample copies of books, hand them out to the groups. Give each group a few different books, allow time for the group members to look over and discuss the books, and then have the groups exchange their books with other groups. Place a time limit of eight to ten minutes on looking at each set of books before passing them on. A time limit is important because it will keep the students focused.

• If you do not have sample copies, or if you want to expand the scope of the project, suggest that your students visit the Web site http://www.bookhive.org, where they can find information and reviews about books. Perhaps you can schedule time in your school's computer room or library for them to visit this site as a class. Instruct your students to search for books by first clicking on *Find a Book*, then typing the title of the book into *Search Our Book Reviews*, then clicking on the search button. To go to the review, they should click on the title of the book. (*Note:* there are many other Web sites that provide information about books for students. A search using *book lists for kids* will provide several links. However, before directing students to any Web site, visit it yourself first to see if the information it provides is appropriate and easy to access.)

• Hand out copies of Worksheet 33.3: Book Cost and Tally Sheet and go over it with your students. Point out that they must list each book they choose and its author. They must also place a check in the proper column for hardcover or paperback, and include the cost of the book. They must add the costs of the books and subtract the total from their $100 budget. They must not exceed their budget. You may prefer to allow your students to use calculators to tally their costs.

• Remind your students to select a spokesperson to present their group's selections to the class. They should present reasons why they chose the books they did.

Wrap Up

Have the groups share their results with the class.

Extension

Share the lists of books your students selected with your school's librarian. Perhaps arrangements can be made for the library to acquire the books it may not already have.

Encourage your students to read some of the books they selected.

STUDENT GUIDE 33.1

Buying Books for the School Library

Project

Imagine that your class has been given $100 to buy books for the school library. The class will be divided into groups. Each group will recommend novels that they think the class should buy.

Key Steps

1. Divide the tasks of this project among your group's members. One person may make sure the discussion stays on the topic of books. Another person may take notes. Another may keep track of the estimated costs. A fourth may present the group's findings to the class.

2. Group members should share their knowledge of any of the books on the list. If you have sample copies of some of the books, read the back covers and some of the pages. This will help you to decide which books to choose.

3. Decide whether each book should be a hardcover or a paperback. Hardcover books last longer, but paperback books cost less.

4. Keep a running estimate of the cost of the books you choose. This will help you to stay within your budget of $100.

5. Make a list of why you chose each book.

6. After deciding on your books, complete Worksheet 33.3. Use exact prices. Remember that you cannot spend more than $100.

7. Double-check your computation.

8. Pick a group member to present your group's choices to the class. Remember to support your choices with reasons.

Special Tips

- Try to choose books that many people will like. Remember that girls may like different books from what boys like. Write down the reasons you chose a book.

- Maybe visit Web sites that can help you choose books. A good choice is http://www.bookhive.org. Before visiting Web sites, check with your teacher.

To Be Submitted

Your completed worksheet

DATA SHEET 33.2

Book List

Bunnicula: A Rabbit Tale of Mystery by Deborah and James Howe (hardcover, $16.95; paperback, $4.99)

Charlie and the Chocolate Factory by Roald Dahl (hardcover, $15.95; paperback, $6.99)

The Lion, the Witch, and the Wardrobe by C. S. Lewis (hardcover, $16.89; paperback, $8.99)

Harry Potter and the Sorcerer's Stone by J. K. Rowling (hardcover, $22.99; paperback, $8.99)

Charlotte's Web by E. B. White (hardcover, $16.99; paperback, $7.99)

Sarah, Plain and Tall by Patricia MacLachlan (hardcover, $15.99; paperback, $5.99)

Tuck Everlasting by Natalie Babbitt (hardcover, $16.00; paperback, $5.95)

A Wrinkle in Time by Madeleine L'Engle (hardcover, $17.00; paperback, $6.99)

Bridge to Terabithia by Katherine Paterson (hardcover, $15.99; paperback, $6.99)

The Indian in the Cupboard by Lynne Reid Banks (hardcover, $16.95; paperback, $5.99)

Roll of Thunder, Hear My Cry by Mildred Taylor (hardcover, $17.99; paperback, $7.99)

The Secret Garden by Frances Hodgson Burnett (hardcover, $17.99; paperback, $6.99)

Freckle Juice by Judy Blume (hardcover, $17.95; paperback, $4.99)

Dicey's Song by Cynthia Voigt (hardcover, $17.95; paperback, $5.99)

The Wind in the Willows by Kenneth Grahame (hardcover, $19.99; paperback, $5.99)

Encyclopedia Brown, Boy Detective by Donald J. Sobol (hardcover, $13.89; paperback, $5.50)

King of the Wind by Marguerite Henry (hardcover, $10.95; paperback, $5.99)

The Dark Is Rising by Susan Cooper (hardcover, $19.99; paperback, $8.99)

The Slave Dancer by Paula Fox (hardcover, $18.99; paperback, $6.50)

Maniac Magee by Jerry Spinelli (hardcover, $16.99; paperback, $6.99)

Book Cost and Tally Sheet

Complete the following information about your choices of books. Write the title of the book and the name of the author. Place a check in the space for hardcover (H) or paperback (P). Write the price. Add the prices to find the total cost. Subtract the total cost from your budget.

Title of Book	Author	H	P	Price

Total Cost _____

Budget: ___ $100 ___ − Total Cost: _____ = _____

It's About Time

MOST STUDENTS, LIKE MOST ADULTS, live their lives by the clock. We follow schedules based on time, and running late plays havoc with our day. Although often overlooked, time management is an essential skill. In this project, your students will recreate their school schedules right down to the minute.

Goal

Working in pairs or groups of three, students will design a schedule for their school day for a one-week period. Their objective will be to support all the learning they need to do but also provide time for recreation. Upon completion of the project they will share their schedules with the class. *Suggested time:* two to three class periods.

Skills Covered

1. Computing with units of time
2. Evaluating information and making decisions
3. Organizing information in the form of a schedule
4. Using technology (if calculators are used)

Special Materials and Equipment

Rulers. Optional: calculators.

Development

- Before beginning this project, provide your students with the total amount of time allotted to each of their subjects each week. Be sure to include lunch and any special periods such as homeroom or recess. They will also need to know the length of their school day, with starting and ending times.

- Start this project by explaining to your students that they are to work in pairs or groups of three to create what they feel would be their best daily schedule for school, Monday through Friday. Explain that they should strive to create a schedule that gives them enough time for recreation but also supports learning. Although they may design their schedules as they feel best, they must be sure that each subject meets its full weekly time requirements. They must also account for lunch and any special periods.

- Hand out copies of Student Guide 34.1 and review the information it provides with your students. Explain that they should strive to create realistic schedules. For example, although it might seem a good idea to get all of their subjects done before lunch, then finish the day with a final period of gym, most students would find such a day to be extremely tiring. Most would have difficulty concentrating on school work for so long a stretch of time.

- Emphasize to your students that their schedules must fill the school day. They cannot extend or shorten the length of the day. Lunch must be the same amount of time as in their current schedule. However, the time when lunch starts can be changed.

- Suggest to your students that they experiment with rough copies of schedules to find one that works best.

- Caution your students to work accurately with computation of units of time and to double-check their work. If necessary, review adding and subtracting units of time with them. You may wish to provide calculators.

- Distribute copies of Worksheet 34.2: Weekly Schedule. (Have additional copies available in case students make mistakes.) Explain that each day of the week is provided on the worksheet. Students should list the subjects and the times these subjects meet each day. Suggest that they use rulers to draw lines and make a grid for their schedule. Caution them to provide enough space for writing in the subjects, periods, and times.

Wrap Up

Have each group explain their schedule and provide reasons for their design. Discuss how some of the schedules might be improvements over the current schedule. Also discuss why schedules are seldom perfect.

Extensions

Encourage your students to create an individual schedule of their entire day. Discuss how following a schedule can help people manage their time.

STUDENT GUIDE 34.1

It's About Time

Project

You and your partner or group are to create a weekly schedule for your class. You will decide when and how long each subject will be taught each day. You are to try to design a schedule that will make learning easy and that you will like. After you have completed your schedule, you will share it with the class.

Key Steps

1. Discuss with your partner or group what you like and dislike about your current schedule. How might your schedule be improved? Ask yourself questions such as the following:
   - When should math be taught? Before or after lunch?
   - When is the best time for reading?
   - What is the best time for lunch?
   - What subject should be taught first?
   - What subject should be taught last?
2. List your ideas for what a good schedule would be. Remember to include time for lunch and any special periods. You may have a lunch period every day. You may not change the length of your lunch. You may not add time to or subtract time from your school day.
3. Make a rough copy of your schedule on scrap paper. Be sure your computations with units of time are accurate.
4. Write your schedule onto Worksheet 34.2.
5. Be prepared to share your schedule with the class. Explain why you made your schedule the way you did.

Special Tip

- You may change the length of time a subject meets per day. The time must be practical. Each subject must meet the total number of weekly minutes it meets in your current schedule. An average math class might run 45 minutes. A 10-minute math class is not practical.

To Be Submitted

Your completed worksheet

WORKSHEET 34.2

Weekly Schedule

Create a weekly school schedule. Start at the beginning of each day. Write the time range (for example, Math, 9:20–10:05) for each subject that will be taught. Remember to include the time for lunch and any special periods. Use a ruler to draw lines between periods.

Monday	Tuesday	Wednesday	Thursday	Friday

Numbers
in the News

NUMBERS PLAY A PROMINENT ROLE in many newspaper and magazine articles by communicating ideas and supporting facts. Many of us do not even think about how much of the information is based on numbers. In this project your students will find out just how important numbers are to the news.

Goal

Working in groups of three or four, students will find articles in newspapers and magazines that use numbers to communicate, support, and expand ideas. They will create a collage of articles, then choose one article from their collage and write a summary of it, noting the importance of numbers in the article. *Suggested time:* two to three class periods.

Skills Covered

1. Various math skills depending on the content of the articles
2. Recognizing the wide use of numbers in written material
3. Connecting mathematics to daily events
4. Communicating mathematical ideas

Special Materials and Equipment

Newspapers and old magazines, scissors, poster paper, glue, transparent tape, rulers, and markers.

Development

- Before starting this project, collect old newspapers and magazines. (Be sure to tear off any address labels to protect privacy.) Try to gather publications that are geared to the level and abilities of your students. Magazines designed for classroom use are particularly good choices for this project, as are general-interest publications. Depending on the abilities of your students, you might consider using *USA Today*, which usually contains graphs and tables.

- Begin the project by explaining to your students that they are to work in groups. They are to create a collage of newspaper and magazine articles that use math and numbers to communicate information. Explain that many articles rely on numbers to convey ideas and facts. Good examples are articles about sports. Numbers and statistics are often essential parts of articles about athletes, teams, or specific sports events. Explain that on completion of the collage students are to choose an entire article and write a summary of it, noting how math is used to communicate ideas in the article. They will share their collage and summary with the class.

- Hand out copies of Student Guide 35.1 and review the information it contains with your students. Make sure your students understand that they are to find articles that depend on numbers to communicate information. Numbers should be essential to the article. Emphasize that without numbers to support their ideas, these articles would not provide much information.

- Distribute copies of newspapers and magazines. Caution your students to check the articles carefully. A quick glance at an article might overlook the numbers in it.

- Hand out copies of Worksheet 35.2: Math Makes the News. Note that answering the questions on the worksheet will help students to clarify their ideas for summarizing an article. They should use the information they write on the worksheet as the foundation of their summary. Make sure they understand the terms on the worksheet. For example, *event* refers to the subject of the article. The summary itself should be written on a separate sheet of paper.

- Depending on the level and abilities of your students, you may wish to explain that the worksheet contains the five *W*'s (*Who? What? When? Where?* and *Why?*), which serve as the foundation of the typical newspaper article. Answering these questions about any event results in a significant amount of information.

- Encourage your students to be creative in designing their collages. They should cut out the articles neatly and arrange them in an attractive manner on poster paper.

- Explain to your students that they should choose one article that relies on numbers and summarize it.

Wrap Up

Provide time for your students to show their collages to the class. They should also share their summaries. Discuss how important numbers are to the articles presented.

Extension

Encourage your students to listen to TV or radio newscasts for the ways in which numbers are used in reporting the news. Discuss their findings in class.

STUDENT GUIDE 35.1

Numbers in the News

Project

Your group will make a collage of articles that use numbers in some way. You will cut out articles from newspapers and magazines. You will then choose one of the articles and write a summary of it. In your summary you will explain how numbers are important to the article.

Key Steps

1. Discuss with your group how numbers are used in newspaper and magazine articles. An article about a sports team might include its won-lost record. An article about a snowstorm might include how many inches of snow fell. An article about a school might include the number of students who attend it.

2. Divide newspaper sections and magazines among the group's members. This will make your search for articles easier and faster.

3. Discuss with your group the articles you find. Decide which ones you want to use for your collage. Also decide which article you want to summarize.

4. Neatly cut out articles that show the use of numbers.

5. Arrange the articles in an attractive manner on your poster paper. Glue the clippings to the paper only after you are pleased with the arrangement.

6. Write a title for your collage.

7. For the article you have decided to summarize, answer the questions on Worksheet 35.2. Use the answers to help you write your summary. Write the summary on a separate sheet of paper.

8. Be prepared to share your collage and summary with the class.

Special Tips

- Scan articles to look for numbers. When you find numbers, read the article to see how the numbers are used in it.
- Choose only articles that use numbers to support ideas.

To Be Submitted

Your completed worksheet

Your collage and written summary

Name _____   Date _____

Math Makes the News

Answer the following questions about your article:

1. What is the title of the article? _____

2. Who is the author? _____

3. In which newspaper or magazine did the article appear? _____

   _____

4. What is its date of publication? _____

5. When did the event take place? _____

6. Where did the event take place? _____

7. Who was involved? _____

8. What happened? _____

   _____

   _____

9. Why did the event happen? _____

   _____

   _____

10. How do numbers help make the article meaningful?

   _____

   _____

A Class Math Tournament

MOST STUDENTS ENJOY COMPETITIONS. Whether winning a rousing game of soccer, scoring high at a gymnastics meet, beating an opponent in a video game, or excelling at some other event, competition can be exciting and satisfying. In this project, your students will channel their competitive spirits—and mathematical knowledge—into a class math tournament.

Goal

Working in teams of three to six, students will participate in a math tournament. They will both prepare and answer questions for the tournament. *Suggested time: three to four class periods.*

Skills Covered

Various math skills depending on the questions asked during the tournament.

Special Materials and Equipment

4-inch-by-6-inch index cards. Optional: a different color marker for each team, and a stopwatch, digital clock, or egg timer for keeping time.

Development

• A class math tournament is not difficult to organize and implement, and it may assume a variety of forms. Following is a summary of a basic plan you may use. Divide your students into four or eight groups, or teams. Four or eight teams will allow pairs of teams to play each other, resulting in a straightforward elimination. Note the schemes that follow. The letters indicate teams.

> *Four teams:* A plays B and C plays D. Assume that A and D win. These teams then play each other to determine the winner of the tournament.

> *Eight teams:* A plays B, C plays D, E plays F, and G plays H. Assume the winners are B, D, F, and G. In the next round, B plays D and F plays G. The winners are B and G. These teams then play each other to determine the overall winner.

• This project is most beneficial when students help generate the math problems for the tournament. Prior to starting the project you should decide what materials your students may use to generate problems. You may, for example, prefer that they use the current unit of study, or you may instruct them to use the skills and concepts taught in the last several chapters of their textbooks. To ensure that your students generate reasonable problems, tell them to model their problems on the problems that appear in chapter reviews of their text. Having them write the problems that will be used during the tournament serves a dual purpose. Not only do they generate a variety of problems, but by writing the problems themselves they are simultaneously reviewing material and preparing themselves for the tournament. Be sure to check all of the student problems before the tournament begins. Make certain that they are appropriate and that the answers are correct. Problems that are too easy or too difficult will only undermine the fairness of the competition. We suggest that you also write problems for the tournament. Generating ten to fifteen problems of your own will enable you to make sure that necessary skills are addressed and will provide a greater pool of problems for the tournament.

• There are many ways you can conduct a round of the tournament, and you should implement the competition in the way that best satisfies the needs and abilities of your students and your teaching situation. The following suggestions will work well for most classes:

○ Set up two long tables (or push desks together) so that each team faces the other. We recommend that you be the moderator. As the moderator, you will ask the questions. Having your students write the math problems that you approved on index cards makes it easy for you to shuffle the questions so that they come up randomly. (You should write your problems on index cards too.) Instructing your students to name their teams and to write the team's name in the top left corner of each card enables you to avoid asking students a question that they themselves have generated. For example, if Team A is playing Team B and a question written by either of the teams comes up, simply place the index card face down and go to another question. (Placing the card face down allows you later to show that the question on the card was indeed generated by one of the teams and that you did not simply choose to reject the card, thereby making the competition unfair. Be aware that some students may ask about this.)

- Before starting a round, shuffle the index cards. To decide which team begins you may toss a coin. Choose a card and ask the question of the team that goes first. Read the question slowly and clearly so that students have time to write down numbers or other necessary information on scrap paper. You may need to read the question twice and perhaps clarify a part of it a third time, but you should limit the number of times you repeat any question. The team must answer within a time limit. A stop watch, egg timer, or digital clock is useful for keeping time. Base the time limit on your students' abilities and on the difficulty of the questions. Thirty seconds to a minute is a good limit.

- Once the question is asked, team members may confer with one another. They may use scrap paper, but calculators should not be permitted. A team gets only one chance to answer correctly. A correct answer receives one point, an incorrect answer receives no points. In the case of a correct answer, choose another card and direct the next question to the second team. In the case of an incorrect answer, the second team gets a chance to answer the original question correctly. If they do, they receive the point. The next question then goes to the first team. The process continues in this manner until each team gets a chance to answer up to five questions. At that point, the team with more points wins. The round ends early if it is clear that one team has already won. For example, if after asking each team three questions one team leads 3 to 0, the other team cannot win.

- When there is a tie after each team has answered five questions, ask another question. Now both teams must answer the same question at the same time. The team that answers the question correctly first wins. If neither team answers correctly, continue asking questions until a team wins. The winners of the first round then go on to play each other in a second round.

• This description assumes that you are the moderator and that only two teams are playing at the same time. The rest of the class is the audience. You can expand this format and have four or more teams playing at the same time. In this case you might simply allow opposing teams to draw the cards from a central pile and ask each other questions. (Be sure to remove any questions generated by either of the teams before play begins.) Note, however, that several teams playing at once can be a management challenge, especially if your class has energetic students.

• Start this project by explaining to your students that they will work in teams and that each team will compete in a class math tournament. Describe the format you will use, including the types of questions that will be asked, the amount of time allotted for giving an answer, and the scoring procedure. Also note that students will create some of the questions and that you will create the others.

• Hand out copies of Student Guide 36.1 and review the information it contains with your students. Especially discuss the strategies they should consider.

Hands-On Math Projects

- Offer guidelines for the questions that students will generate. For example, you may direct them to create problems based on only certain topics, on the last three chapters of your text, or on all the material covered since the beginning of the school year. Emphasize that they should model their problems on the problems found in their text, particularly those in the chapter and unit reviews. Explain that you will check their problems before using them in the tournament.

- You may want to suggest that your students create names for their teams. This can build enthusiasm.

- Distribute copies of Worksheet 36.2: Problems for a Class Math Tournament. Instruct your students to create five problems and write them on the worksheet along with the answers. When they are done, they should double-check their work, then hand in the worksheet to you so that you may check the problems and answers for accuracy.

- Explain that after you have checked their problems you will hand the worksheets back to the students and they will rewrite the problems on index cards. The problems and answers should be written on one side of the card, one problem per card. The question should be written in the middle of the card and the answer should be written in the lower right-hand corner. The team's name should be written in the upper left-hand corner of the card. As noted earlier, this will make it easy to avoid giving a team a question they wrote. You may suggest that the teams use a marker to highlight their name. A different color for each team will help the name to stand out.

Wrap Up

On with the tournament!

Extension

Continue playing and allow teams that did not get a chance to play each other in the first round to square off. You should have enough questions left over, but in case you run short you can always take some from your math text or a math resource book.

STUDENT GUIDE 36.1

A Class Math Tournament

Project

Your team will take part in a class math tournament. In preparation for the tournament you will create five math problems. Your teacher will also provide problems. Other teams must solve your problems and the problems of your teacher. Your team must solve problems created by other teams and your teacher.

Key Steps

1. Choose a name for your team. Try to choose a name that has something to do with math, for example, *The Great Dividers* or *The Multiples.*

2. Follow your teacher's guidelines for the types of math problems to create. Think about the different kinds of math problems you have solved. Check the review problems in your math book.

3. Discuss the types of problems you will create with your group. Create different kinds of problems, such as addition, subtraction, multiplication, and division problems. Maybe you will write word problems. Maybe you will create problems based on formulas.

4. Also write the answers to your problems.

5. Complete Worksheet 36.2. Hand it in to your teacher for his or her approval.

6. After your teacher approves your problems, rewrite them on index cards. Write one problem on each card. Write your team's name in the top left of the card, write the problem neatly in the middle, and write the answer in the lower right-hand corner.

Special Tips

- Double-check the answers to your problems. All team members should solve the problems before you hand them in to your teacher. If team members get different answers, the team must find the errors and correct them.

- Use the following strategies to help you win the math tournament:

  ○ Your team should have enough pencils and plenty of paper ready.

  ○ Listen to the problem carefully. Write down the information you need to solve it.

  ○ When given a problem, every team member should try to solve it.

  ○ Work quietly and quickly. Noise will distract you and others from your work.

  ○ Compare answers. If everyone has the same answer, the team is probably right.

  ○ If some people have different answers, double-check the work.

  ○ Remember that you have a time limit. Maybe one team member can keep track of the time.

  ○ Your team can give only one answer.

To Be Submitted

Your completed worksheet

Your index cards with problems

Problems for a Class Math Tournament

Write five problems to be used in your class math tournament.

1.   Answer: _____

2.   Answer: _____

3.   Answer: _____

4.   Answer: _____

5.   Answer: _____

Creating a Review for a Math Test

MOTIVATING YOUR STUDENTS to review and prepare for a math test can be a demanding task. When the next math test approaches, rather than simply assigning review material, assign this project that requires students to create their own review problems.

Goal

Working in groups of three or four, students will write a review for an upcoming test. They must also provide an answer key for their problems. *Suggested time:* two to three class periods.

Skills Covered

1. Various math skills depending on the unit of study
2. Using technology (if calculators or computers are used)

Special Materials and Equipment

Black pens, correction fluid, and 8½-inch-by-11-inch white paper. Optional: calculators, computers, and printers.

Development

- At least a few days before beginning this project, consider how you will use the reviews your students create. You may make copies of each group's review and distribute them to the class to use in preparation for the test, or you may select some problems from each of the student reviews and compile a review of your own. You may also add problems to those of your students to ensure that the review addresses all of the skills and concepts that will be on the test.

- Decide how many and the type of problems that students should include in their reviews. Eight to ten problems per group is a good goal. Fewer than eight may not provide enough problems for practice, and more than ten may be too challenging for some students.

- Finally, write a list of skills and concepts that your students should know for the upcoming test. This list can serve as a guide for your students as they create their review problems.

- Start the project by explaining to your students that they will work in groups and create review sheets for an upcoming math test. Provide them with a list of skills and concepts that the problems in their reviews must address. Explain whether you will photocopy each group's review sheets and hand out the copies to the class or incorporate some of each group's problems into a review of your own. (This second plan gives you greater control of the content of the review material.)

- Distribute copies of Student Guide 37.1 and review the information on it with your students. Note that they should model their review problems on the kinds of problems they have been doing for class and homework. Encourage them to create the kinds of problems they think will be on the test.

- Hand out copies of Data Sheet 37.2: Tips for Writing Review Problems, and discuss the information on it with your students. Emphasize that following the guidelines will help them to write useful review problems.

- Depending on the abilities of your students and their access to computers, you may encourage them to write their review problems on a computer. Most word processing software contains math symbols that allow users to write simple equations and can also generate tables, charts, and graphs. This approach, however, may be challenging for younger students.

- If you plan to photocopy the review sheets created by each group, remind your students to write their problems clearly in black ink on white paper. This will result in clear copies. Correction fluid can be used to rectify mistakes.

- Emphasize the importance of accuracy. Answer keys must be correct. You may suggest that your students use calculators to double-check their work.

- Set the deadline for the completion of the review sheets a few days before the test date. This will provide you with the time necessary to check your students' problems, finalize their reviews or include some of their problems with yours, make copies, and distribute the copies to the class.

Wrap Up

Have your students use the reviews to prepare for the upcoming test.

Extension

Make writing review problems for math tests an ongoing activity. This will help to improve your students' study skills.

STUDENT GUIDE 37.1

Creating a Review for a Math Test

Project

Your group will write review problems for a math test.

Key Steps

1. Think about the kinds of problems that might be on the math test. Think about the kinds of problems you work on in class and for homework. Use these problems as models for your review problems.

2. Discuss the types of problems your review should have.

3. Use the tips on Data Sheet 37.2 to help you create review problems.

4. Write your problems on a white sheet of paper. Leave enough space to work out the problems. Use black ink.

5. Include the answers for all of your problems on the back of your review sheet. Double-check your work.

Special Tip

- Write clear directions for your problems. The directions should state exactly what students are to do.

To Be Submitted

Your review sheet

DATA SHEET 37.2

Tips for Writing Review Problems

The following tips can help you write review problems for a math test:

1. The problems should focus on the math skills that will be tested.

2. Do not create problems that are too easy or too hard. Try to pick problems that will help you and other students prepare for the test.

3. Use different kinds of problems in your review. You might include some of the following:

   - Computation
   - Estimation
   - Multiple choice
   - True or false
   - Fill in the blank
   - Short answer
   - Answers that require written explanations

4. If possible, use word problems in your review.

5. Try using multistep problems.

6. Think about using tables, charts, or graphs with your problems.

7. Be sure that all of the information in your problems is accurate. Also be sure to include all information needed for solving each problem.

8. Include an answer key.

The Presenters

THE ABILITY TO COMMUNICATE is an essential skill for students as well as adults. People who can express themselves clearly have an advantage over those who have trouble formulating and sharing ideas. This project gives your students practice in presenting information to an audience composed of their classmates.

Goal

Working in groups of four or five, students will present a math topic to the class. They will include posters, illustrations, charts, tables, or graphs to support their topics. *Suggested time:* three to four class periods.

Skills Covered

1. Various math skills depending on the topics presented
2. Researching topics in mathematics
3. Organizing math information
4. Using math to communicate ideas
5. Using technology (if computers are used)

255

Special Materials and Equipment

Will vary depending on the topics presented, but some or all of the following are likely to be needed: math reference books, index cards, poster paper, rulers, markers, and crayons. Optional: computers with Internet access.

Development

- Before beginning this project, check Data Sheet 38.2: Possible Topics for a Math Presentation, and decide which of the topics are suitable for your students. Perhaps they all are. You may wish to incorporate additional topics that are stressed in your curriculum.

- Because research is an important part of this project, consider scheduling time in your school's library for your students to gather information about their topics. Ask the librarian to set aside math reference books that will be helpful. You might also consider scheduling time in your school's computer room so that your students may conduct research online.

- Finally, you should decide how long you would like your students' presentations to run. Three to five minutes is probably enough time for most topics.

- Start this project by explaining to your students that they will work in groups and will present a topic in math to the class. They will need to research their topic, organize information, and make an oral presentation.

- Hand out copies of Student Guide 38.1 and review the information on it with your students. Mention how long their presentations should run. Also note that they may want to create posters, illustrations, charts, tables, or graphs to support their ideas. In some cases they may want to use the board to show examples.

- Distribute copies of Data Sheet 38.2 and review the topics with your students. Suggest that before choosing a topic they do preliminary research on several. This will help them to find the topics that will be most interesting to them. They should be required to check with you for your approval of a topic before they begin their actual research. This gives you the opportunity to steer a group away from a topic you feel might be too complicated for them, as well as to prevent two groups from researching the same topic. This project is most beneficial when each group presents a different topic.

- Instruct your students to research their topics thoroughly. To present their topics to the class, students must understand their material. They should consult math reference books as well as their textbooks. Depending on their abilities and their access to computers, encourage your students to research their topics online. For example, searching on *mathematical palindromes* will result in links to numerous Web sites. As your students visit these Web sites, provide guidance as necessary. Some Web sites might be too advanced for young students.

- Hand out copies of Worksheet 38.3: Presentation Planner. Explain that writing the main ideas for the introduction, body, and conclusion of their presentation will help them to organize their information in a logical manner. Note that they should also list any materials they will create to support their ideas, as well as materials they will need for their presentation.

• Suggest to your students that the materials they use to support their ideas might include posters, illustrations, charts, tables, or graphs. For some topics—for example, square numbers—they may find it helpful to write examples on the board. For other topics, such as a presentation on the abacas, showing an example of a real abacas (perhaps one is tucked away in the math department) can make the presentation more interesting.

• Emphasize to your students that they must inform you of any special materials they will need. They should do this well in advance of their presentation.

• Instruct your students that as they prepare for their presentations they should write notes on index cards. Referring to their notes during their presentations will help them to remember to include all of the important points.

Wrap Up

Have your students present their topics to the class. Encourage a question-and-answer session after each presentation.

Extension

Arrange for your students to present their topics to students in other classes. This is a great way for them to hone their oral presentation skills as well as to share information about math with others.

STUDENT GUIDE 38.1

The Presenters

Project

Your group will present a topic in math to the class.

Key Steps

1. Check Data Sheet 38.2 for ideas. Discuss any of the topics you already know something about.

2. Research different topics to find one that interests your group. Use math reference books for your research. Also check your math textbook for information.

3. Once you have chosen a topic, learn as much about it as you can and take careful notes.

4. To help you plan and organize your presentation, complete Worksheet 38.3.

5. Support all main ideas with details. Include examples, posters, illustrations, charts, tables, or graphs.

6. Let your teacher know if you need any special materials for your presentation.

7. Decide which group members will present your topic. You may decide on one or two people. You may have everyone take part in presenting your information.

8. Write the main ideas and important details of your topic on index cards. Use your index cards during your presentation. Practice giving your presentation.

9. During your presentation, speak clearly. If you write examples on the board, be sure that your letters and numbers are neat. Display any posters, illustrations, or other materials so that everyone can see them.

10. Be ready to answer any questions your classmates may have.

Special Tips

- If possible, check for information about your topic online.
- Divide the work between the members of your group.

To Be Submitted

Your completed worksheet

Your index cards with notes for your presentation

Any other materials such as posters, illustrations, or charts

DATA SHEET 38.2

Possible Topics for a Math Presentation

Mathematical palindromes

Perfect, abundant, and deficient numbers

Square numbers

Prime and composite numbers

Divisibility rules

Fibonacci series

Bases

Scientific notation

Ancient number systems

The abacus

Math tricks

Logic puzzles

Sudoku puzzles

Math shortcuts

Number lines

Venn diagrams

Magic squares

Pentominoes

Tessellations

The golden ratio

Pascal's triangle

Tangrams

Reflections

Rotations

Möbius strip

Nets

Polyhedrons

Euler's Formula

Others:

_____

_____

_____

_____

_____

_____

_____

_____

WORKSHEET 38.3

Presentation Planner

1. List the main ideas of the introduction of your presentation.

   _____

   _____

   _____

2. List the main ideas of the body of your presentation.

   _____

   _____

   _____

   _____

   _____

   _____

   _____

   _____

3. List the main ideas of the conclusion of your presentation.

   _____

   _____

   _____

4. List any materials you will create (for example, posters or illustrations) to support your ideas.

   _____

   _____

5. List any special materials you will need for your presentation.

   _____

   _____

Setting Up a Math Portfolio

A MATH PORTFOLIO CONTAINS EXAMPLES of a student's work collected over a given period. It may include assignments, quizzes, tests, reports, projects, and other materials that show his or her progress in learning math. A good portfolio should not only demonstrate an understanding of concepts and skills but should also reveal a student's attitude toward and appreciation of math. Portfolios can confirm far more about a student's overall achievement than daily work and assessments.

Although portfolios can be specialized as a *work portfolio* or an *assessment portfolio*, we recommend that you maintain general portfolios for your students so that various examples of their math work may be included.

As useful as they are for teachers, math portfolios are also helpful to students. As the year progresses, your students may review their portfolios. Many will be surprised, and pleased, with their achievement in math.

Goal

Working individually, students will maintain a math portfolio. *Suggested time:* one class period to introduce and start the project, then ongoing updates and periodic reviews throughout the year.

Skills Covered

1. Various math skills depending on the material placed in the portfolios
2. Organizing information

Special Materials and Equipment

A large folder or heavy envelope for each student, a cardboard box or milk crate for storing the portfolios in class, and black markers to write the students' names on their portfolios.

Development

- Before starting this project, decide how long your students will maintain their portfolios. Consider extending this project for a marking period, for a semester, or for the entire school year. Also decide what types of work your students may choose to include in their portfolios. Data Sheet 39.2: Math Portfolio Guidelines offers some examples. You may add to the list.

- Although you may require your students to place specific materials in their portfolios, you should also give them the opportunity to select other examples of work they feel reflects their achievement, insight, or appreciation of math. Giving students the chance to select material allows them to assume ownership of their portfolios and can enhance their enthusiasm.

- Because most items that go into a portfolio have already been graded, we recommend that you do not grade portfolios. The greatest value of a portfolio is its demonstration of a student's growth in and mastery of math. If your students feel that their portfolios will be graded, they may be tempted to stuff them with materials they feel will boost their grades and to ignore important material they feel may result in a poor grade. A good example here is a response that shows insight into a tough problem but that may not be written particularly well or may contain minor errors. Some students may feel that their errors will detract from their grade and therefore not include this material.

- Begin this project by explaining to your students that each of them will maintain a math portfolio. Explain that a portfolio shows examples of their work and allows you and the students to review their work and note their progress as the year goes on.

- Hand out copies of Student Guide 39.1 and review the information it contains with your students. Make sure they understand what they are to do. If they have never maintained a math portfolio before, they will probably have several questions.

- Hand out copies of Data Sheet 39.2 and discuss the information on it. The first part details the kinds of work your students may place in their portfolios. The second part notes skills and traits that their portfolios should show about them. Encourage your students to select examples of their work to place in their portfolios. Suggest that they choose different kinds of work that show their growth and understanding of math. You may find it necessary to work with some students during the selection process.

- Distribute large folders or envelopes. Explain to your students that these will serve as their portfolios. Have students use markers to print their names clearly in the top left-hand corner of their portfolios. Store the portfolios in class in a cardboard box or milk crate. (Allowing students to take their portfolios home risks not having the portfolios come back.)

- Encourage your students to file their own work. Instruct them to keep their portfolios in alphabetical order in the portfolio box. You should remind them when you want them to place specific kinds of their work in their portfolios, for example, unit tests.

- Instruct your students to date all of the work that goes into their portfolios. They should arrange their work in order according to date. This makes it easier to retrieve specific papers.

- Suggest that your students create a contents page for their portfolios. The contents page should be placed in the front of the portfolio and should be updated periodically.

- If over time the number of pages makes the portfolios too large, suggest that students go through their portfolios and keep only what they feel is their best work.

- Explain to your students that you will periodically review their portfolios. Encourage them to review their work as well. They will likely be surprised by all of the math they have learned.

Wrap Up

Review portfolios with individual students. Discuss their progress in math and offer suggestions for continued improvement.

Extension

Share the portfolios of each student with his or her parents at conference time.

STUDENT GUIDE 39.1

Setting Up a Math Portfolio

Project

You will start and keep a math portfolio. You will place examples of your math work in your portfolio and review it throughout the year.

Key Steps

1. Write your name on your portfolio.
2. Read Data Sheet 39.2. It lists the kinds of work you may put in your portfolio. It also explains what the work in your portfolio should show about you. Think about the kinds of work you would like to include. Be sure to include all of the work your teacher asks you to put in your portfolio.
3. Make sure your name and the date is on all of your work.
4. Place your work in your portfolio in order of date.
5. Write a contents page for your portfolio. Update your contents page as needed.

Special Tips

- Put only math work in your portfolio.
- Staple together the pages of long assignments so that they do not become separated.

To Be Submitted

Your portfolio

DATA SHEET 39.2

Math Portfolio Guidelines

Following are examples of the kinds of work you may include in your portfolio:

- Homework
- Quizzes and tests
- Reports
- Notes for math projects and oral presentations
- Examples of group work
- Solutions to word problems (showing all of the work)
- Written explanations of math concepts
- An entry from your math journal (if you have one)

The work in your portfolio should show that you

1. Are accurate in solving problems
2. Understand math concepts
3. Understand and apply math rules
4. Understand and use math vocabulary
5. Gather and organize data to solve problems
6. Draw correct conclusions from data
7. Support conclusions with evidence
8. Understand word problems
9. Use many different strategies for solving problems
10. Use models to show math concepts
11. Use technology
12. Relate math to your life

My Best Day
in Math Class

AS YOUR STUDENTS LOOK BACK OVER the year in math, they will realize that they studied many topics and learned many new concepts and skills. For this project, your students are to reflect on what they feel was their best day in your math class. This is a fine project to conclude the year.

Goal

Working individually, students will write and illustrate an essay about their best day in math. *Suggested time:* two class periods.

Skills Covered

1. Various math skills depending on the content of the students' writing
2. Using writing to communicate mathematical ideas
3. Creating an illustration to express ideas about math
4. Using technology (if computers are used)

Special Materials and Equipment

Drawing paper, rulers, markers, crayons, and colored pencils. Optional: computers and printers.

Development

- Summarize with your students the many topics they studied this year in math. Mention that although they may have found some topics to be challenging, they probably found others easy to understand. Some days certainly were better than others; for this project they are to focus on what they consider to be their best day in math class.

- Start this project by explaining to your students that they will work individually. They are to reflect on their best day in math class. Perhaps this was a time they solved a really hard problem, earned an *A* on a test of material they initially found to be difficult, or experienced one of those ah-ha moments when their understanding of something new became crystal clear.

- Distribute copies of Student Guide 40.1 and review the information on it with your students. Note especially that both their writing and their illustration should focus on their best day.

- Hand out copies of Worksheet 40.2: Remembering My Best Day. Explain that answering the questions on the worksheet will help students formulate their ideas for writing.

- Encourage your students to write a rough copy first, then to revise and polish their work. Depending on their abilities, and their access to computers, you might encourage them to write their essays on the computer. This will make revision easier.

- Note that their illustrations should support the main ideas in their writing. Although their illustrations need not be overly complex, they should express the student's ideas clearly. The illustrations should be done on separate sheets of paper and attached to their written account.

Wrap Up

Conduct a discussion about the best days in math class this year. Display the work of your students.

Extension

Discuss with your students how they can help ensure that their next year in math will be productive and enjoyable.

My Best Day in Math Class

Project

You are to write and illustrate an essay about your best day in math class this year.

Key Steps

1. Think about the topics you studied in math this year. Which ones did you enjoy most?

2. Think about a day in math class that you were at your best. List ideas about this best day.

3. Complete Worksheet 40.2. Completing the worksheet will help you to clarify your thoughts.

4. Write an essay about your best day. Revise your writing.

5. Draw a picture that supports your writing. Your picture should highlight an important part of your best day. Add color to make your picture attractive.

6. Attach your picture to your finished essay.

7. Be prepared to discuss your best day with the class.

Special Tips

- Be sure to use correct grammar and punctuation.
- Write and revise your essay on a computer if possible.

To Be Submitted

Your completed worksheet

Your essay and illustration

Remembering My Best Day

Answer each of the following questions. Use the answers to help you write about your best day in math this year.

1. What was your best day in math this year? _____
   _____

2. What were you working on? _____
   _____
   _____
   _____

3. Who (if anyone) was working with you? _____
   _____
   _____

4. Describe any problem(s) you were having. _____
   _____
   _____
   _____
   _____

5. How did you solve the problem(s)? _____
   _____
   _____
   _____
   _____

6. Why was this your best day in math class? _____
   _____
   _____
   _____
   _____